BRAVE animal stories for Kids

Shirley Raye Redmond

HARVEST HOUSE PUBLISHERS
EUGENE, OREGON

T0016915

Published in association with Books & Such Literary Management, www.booksandsuch.com.

Cover design, illustrations, and hand lettering by Kristi Smith—Juicebox Designs
Interior design by KUHN Design Group

For bulk, special sales, or ministry purchases, please call 1-800-547-8979.
Email: Customerservice@hhpbooks.com

This logo is a federally registered trademark of the Hawkins Children's LLC. Harvest House Publishers, Inc., is the exclusive licensee of this trademark.

Brave Animal Stories for Kids

Copyright © 2023 by Shirley Raye Redmond
Published by Harvest House Publishers
Eugene, Oregon 97408
www.harvesthousepublishers.com

ISBN 978-0-7369-8714-1 (pbk.)
ISBN 978-0-7369-8715-8 (eBook)

Library of Congress Control Number: 2022948942

Printed in the United States of America

23 24 25 26 27 28 29 30 31 / BP / 10 9 8 7 6 5 4 3 2 1

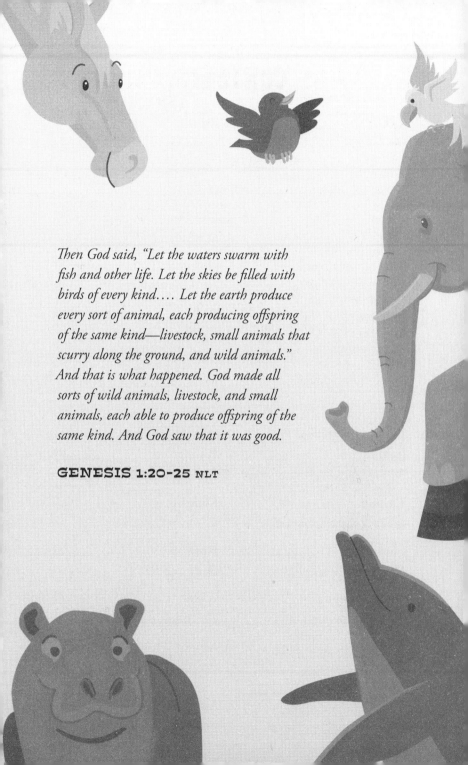

Then God said, "Let the waters swarm with fish and other life. Let the skies be filled with birds of every kind.... Let the earth produce every sort of animal, each producing offspring of the same kind—livestock, small animals that scurry along the ground, and wild animals." And that is what happened. God made all sorts of wild animals, livestock, and small animals, each able to produce offspring of the same kind. And God saw that it was good.

GENESIS 1:20-25 NLT

CONTENTS

INTRODUCTION

Heroes give us hope. But not all heroes are human. Some have fur, paws, beaks, or hooves. In the Bible, the Lord used animals to serve His purpose, such as feeding Elijah with the help of ravens and exhorting wicked Balaam through his donkey. God's creatures have often shown remarkable courage and devotion in the face of danger. Animals have saved lives, prevented harm, and even predicted health-related incidents. When instinct tells them to flee, animal heroes have exhibited remarkable bravery in their efforts to save others.

Courageous cats, devoted dogs, plucky parrots, and dedicated dolphins—no creature is too small or too humble to be employed by God. Author Harriet Beecher Stowe once said, "We should remember in our dealings with animals that they are a sacred trust to us from our heavenly Father." Recognizing that animals are capable of compassion and devoted service should inspire the same in us.

ROSELLE

Hero of 9/11

2001

For Michael Hingson and his guide dog, a yellow Labrador retriever named Roselle, September 11, 2001, began just like any other workday in New York City. As usual, Roselle had safely led Michael to his office in the World Trade Center. Because Michael had been blind from birth, he had never been able to admire the view of the city skyline from his window on the seventy-eighth floor in the North Tower. As he prepared for a business meeting, a hijacked jetliner crashed into the building. Following the loud boom, a violent tremor shook the office. The tower began to tilt and sway. Some people screamed and others cried. One of Michael's coworkers mentioned the smoke and fire outside the window and the millions of pieces of paper floating through the air.

Michael knew they had to get out of the damaged building. Roselle, who'd been snoozing under Michael's desk, didn't panic. She knew what to do. With Michael gripping her harness, she calmly led him down the emergency stairs. It was hot, and thick smoke and the nauseating smell of jet fuel made it hard to breathe. When frightened people tried to push past them, afraid the lights would go out in the stairwell, Michael urged them not to panic.

Roselle would lead the way. There were more than a thousand steps. Michael and Roselle descended one at a time.

When they reached the lobby, they hurried outside. Michael tried to call his wife to let her know he was okay. Just then Michael heard a deafening roar like a freight train coming toward him. A policeman shouted for everyone to run fast—one of the towers was collapsing. The air became filled with toxic dust and chunks of debris. Michael choked and gasped. He could hardly breathe. Roselle calmly led him through the rubble-filled streets to shelter down in the subway.

Thousands of people died that tragic day, including the brave firefighters who gave Roselle a friendly pat on the head as they passed her on the stairs going up to fight the flames. Michael credited his loyal companion with saving his life and the lives of others. For her heroic efforts, Roselle received the Award for Canine Excellence from the American Kennel Club in 2002.

SOMETHING TO THINK ABOUT

How do you think it would feel to survive an incident like the one that occurred on 9/11? It's easy to become frightened or discouraged by such events. Just remember, God sees the big picture. He can turn tragedies into triumphs.

Dear heavenly Father, sometimes I worry about scary things happening in the world. Touch me with Your peace. Help me to realize that with You, I don't need to fear anything. In Jesus's name, amen.

SERGEANT RECKLESS

Korean Warhorse

1953

Reckless was a small Korean mare bred to be a racehorse. Instead, she became a Marine! A Korean stable boy, desperate for cash, offered to sell her for $250. He wanted to purchase a prosthetic leg for his sister, who had been seriously injured when she stepped on a land mine. A US Marine commander in need of a pack horse willingly paid the price. The little mare was dubbed "Reckless" when she joined the 5th Marines Recoilless Rifle ("Reckless") Platoon. She was trained to carry ammunition through waterlogged rice paddies and over mountainous terrain not suitable for motorized vehicles. The soldiers taught her to watch out for trip wires and to seek shelter when someone yelled "*Incoming!*"

Reckless loved to eat. The men laughed at the mare's enormous appetite. She enjoyed pancakes, scrambled eggs, and Hershey bars. She ate bowls of shredded wheat and snatched peanut butter sandwiches whenever she had the chance. Once she even ate the lining out of a soldier's combat helmet. She drank coffee but especially loved Coca-Cola. When the weather was cold outside, she'd invade the men's tents to sleep alongside them.

Reckless won their respect, however, during the brutal battle for Outpost Vegas in the Korean War. She made fifty-one trips up and down a steep hill hauling nine thousand pounds of ammunition to the front lines. At first, she was accompanied by one of the men. But as the battle raged and more Marines were killed, Reckless made the trek alone. The sight of the mare trudging up the rubble-strewn hill raised the morale of the hard-pressed Marines. She completed most of her trips without a soldier to guide her. Even after being wounded above one eye and in her left flank, brave Reckless pushed onward, remaining steadfast in her duties despite the carnage around her.

After the battle, she became Sergeant Reckless. For the rest of the war, soldiers placed their flak jackets over the beloved mare to prevent injury during bombardments, risking their own lives for her sake. Reckless wasn't a horse, they insisted—she was a fellow Marine! She inspired awe and respect from all who learned of her bravery.

After the war, the men insisted on taking her with them to Camp Pendleton in California. One shipping firm offered her free passage from Korea to San Francisco. She arrived in the United States in November 1954, just in time for the Marine Corps Birthday Ball, where she enjoyed eating cake and all the flower arrangements! When Reckless died in 1968, the grateful Marines buried her with full military honors.

SOMETHING TO THINK ABOUT

Considered America's greatest warhorse, Reckless was recognized at a special ceremony on Capitol Hill in 2019. She was cited for her "absolute dependability."

Could someone describe you as dependable? A dependable person is someone you can count on no matter what. Are you that kind of person?

*Lord, show me how to be the sort of person other
people can trust. In Jesus's name, amen.*

JAMBO

Gorilla Guardian

1986

When five-year-old Levan Merritt leaned over the railing of the gorilla pit at the Jersey Zoo in England, he never imagined he'd fall in. But that's exactly what happened. The twenty-foot drop into the enclosure snapped Levan's arm and fractured his skull. His parents and other spectators watched in horror as seven gorillas lumbered toward the unconscious boy. That's when Jambo, a giant seven-foot silverback, positioned himself between Levan and the other gorillas. Jambo stood over the boy protectively, preventing the others from getting too close. It was almost as though he was signaling them, *Do not touch!*

While Levan's mother cried, the anxious onlookers shouted and screamed. Everyone knew the gorilla could send the unconscious child flying across the enclosure with one swing of his powerful, furry arm. When one of the nervous gorillas paced the enclosure in an aggressive manner, Jambo remained on guard. He leaned in close to sniff Levan's hand. Jambo even stroked the boy's back.

Two brave men, a paramedic and a zoo employee, jumped into the enclosure to rescue Levan. Thanks to Jambo, who led the gorilla band away from Levan, the men were able to get the boy out. The entire incident, captured on video, made prime-time news around the world. Levan spent six weeks in the hospital, recovering from his injuries. He was amazed when he watched Jambo's behavior on video. Only Jambo's caregiver at the zoo was not surprised, insisting that although Jambo had the strength of ten men, he also had the heart of a lamb.

Over the years, a grateful Levan returned to the zoo many times to visit his gorilla guardian. After Jambo died, Levan was invited to cut the ribbon at a celebration following the installment of a bronze statue dedicated to the gentle giant.

SOMETHING TO THINK ABOUT

Jambo is not the only gorilla known to have protected a human child. In 1996, a female lowland gorilla named Binta Jua at the Brookfield Zoo near Chicago, Illinois, cradled an injured three-year-old boy in her arms after he'd fallen into her enclosure. She carried him gently to the doorway and laid him at the feet of the paramedics who had come to rescue the boy.

Has God ever used an animal in your life in an unexpected way? We don't have to understand everything the Lord does. We can be content knowing that it's all a part of His plan for our good and His glory.

Dear Lord, what an amazing Creator You are! There are so many awesome creatures in this world in a wide variety of colors, shapes, and sizes. There are also many different kinds of people. I thank You for making me a part of Your wonderful creation. In Jesus's name, amen.

BING

The Parachute Pup

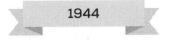

1944

During World War II, some combat dogs were trained to jump from airplanes wearing special parachute harnesses. Airborne troops nicknamed them "para pups." Before being assigned to work with Britain's 13th Parachute Battalion, an Alsatian named Bing attended War Dog Training School. He learned to tolerate loud noises—the roar of airplane engines at full throttle, the whirring of airplane propellers, and the sudden blasts of explosions.

Before jumping from an airplane, Bing was allowed to smell a chunk of meat in his handler's pocket. Then his handler jumped from the plane first. Bing followed after him, his parachute opening automatically as the pup plummeted from the plane. Once he landed, Bing remained still, waiting for his handler to remove the harness. That's when Bing received his reward. The routine was always the same: jump, land, eat. After each successful jump, Bing wagged his tail triumphantly. Sometimes he was dabbed with dark camouflage paint so the enemy couldn't spot him as he jumped from the airplane.

Bing's biggest assignment took place on June 5, 1944—the famous D-Day invasion in Normandy, France. Bing sailed through the sky amid heavy mortar fire. He suffered two deep cuts to his face. His parachute got tangled in a tree. He hung there for hours before his handler could cut him down. Although wounded, Bing remained undaunted. He took his place in line with the rest of the battalion and carried on with the task of safely leading the troops through enemy-held territory. When something seemed wrong, he'd freeze and point his nose toward the danger. He saved the men in his battalion from ambush many times. At night while they slept, Bing kept watch. The troops trusted him and took comfort in his ability to keep them safe while they rested. Many officers firmly believed that sentry dogs were more effective than human guards.

After the war, the heroic hound was returned to his owner in England—a teenager named Betty Fetch. She'd been heartbroken when her parents donated Bing to the war effort. But because of diminishing food rations, her family could no longer feed her pet. Betty was delighted to have her beloved dog home once again. She realized how lucky she was because not all brave war dogs returned home. Many died on the battlefields.

SOMETHING TO THINK ABOUT

In 1947, the People's Dispensary for Sick Animals awarded Bing the Dickin Medal, the United Kingdom's highest honor bestowed upon animals who served the armed forces with valor and distinction. Betty looked on proudly as Bing received his medal. "Valor" means "courage in the face of danger, especially in battle."

The Bible is filled with stories of courageous men and women—like Joshua and Gideon and Deborah and Esther. Do you know anyone, perhaps a military veteran, who has received a medal for valor like Bing did?

Dear Lord, I ask a special prayer for all the people
and animals that serve in our military in the
United States or overseas. Surround them with
Your love and peace. In Jesus's name, amen.

MAGAWA

HeroRAT

2020

When most people see rats, they shudder with distaste. Rats are known to carry diseases and deadly infections. They cause damage in homes, schools, and office buildings. Rats were to blame for the devastating plague known as the Black Death, which raged across the world in the middle 1300s.

But today some special rats are performing a great service. They detect deadly land mines in countries like Angola, Mozambique, Zimbabwe, and Cambodia. It is estimated that there are over one hundred million land mines around the world, posing a threat to both people and animals. Every year 15,000 to 20,000 people are killed or maimed by land mines.

An African giant pouched rat, Magawa was part of a team known as HeroRATs. These large rats weigh more than two pounds and measure twenty-eight inches long. They are native to Africa. Although it might be hard to believe, these rats are intelligent and easy to train. God created them with a keen sense of smell, which enables them to detect underground explosives. Trained by a Belgian not-for-profit organization, Magawa and other HeroRATs work in Africa and Asia. The training is time consuming and difficult. The rats must get used to working with humans and learn to wear a special harness and leash. They must be taught to walk a rope grid.

These rats, which are more effective than dogs at sniffing out land mines and easier to transport from one place to another, do not respond to voice commands. Handlers teach them using a system of clicking sounds. When the rats perform well, they are rewarded with bananas or peanuts. Clever and brave, Magawa could clear an area the size of a tennis court in twenty minutes— far less time than a person with a metal detector. Even if Magawa made a mistake, the rat was so light-footed that when he stepped on a mine, it did not detonate.

In 2020, Magawa became the only rat ever to receive a Gold Medal from the People's Dispensary for Sick Animals. This medal is the United Kingdom's civilian equivalent of the Dickin Medal for military animals. Magawa died peacefully at the age of eight after helping to save hundreds of human lives in Cambodia.

SOMETHING TO THINK ABOUT

Does it surprise you that God can use a rat to perform good deeds? The Lord has often used animals to accomplish His will. He used ravens to feed the prophet Elijah in the wilderness. He had a huge fish swallow Jonah to teach him an important lesson.

The Lord has a role for each of us, no matter how young or small we might be. We simply need to be willing, like the prophet Isaiah, who said to the Lord, "Here am I. Send me" (Isaiah 6:8).

Dear Lord, You are amazing! Thank You for people
and rats and other creatures that help to save the
lives of those in danger. In Jesus's name, amen.

STUBBY

Canine Hero of WWI

1917

Stubby was the most famous dog of World War I, but he wasn't a trained war dog at all. Army private J. Robert Conroy found the stray with the stubby tail roaming the streets of New Haven, Connecticut, and adopted him. The small bull terrier drilled with the troops and even learned to salute with his right paw over his eye. When Conroy completed his military training, he sailed with other American soldiers to France, smuggling Stubby onboard. When the dog was discovered, Stubby's sharp salute won the disapproving officer's respect.

On the battlefield, Stubby quickly grew accustomed to rifle and artillery blasts. Once he fell victim to poisonous gas and almost died. When he recovered, the soldiers rigged a special gas mask for him just like theirs. From then on, Stubby used his keen sense of smell to warn the men about gas attacks. Just one whiff caused him to bark and yelp until the men donned their masks and put one on Stubby too. His hearing was also sharp. He could hear the high-pitched whine of incoming mortar rounds. When Stubby dashed for cover, the soldiers did the same. His timely actions saved their lives.

Once Stubby attacked a German spy sneaking into camp

to map out the Allied positions. He bit the man in the leg and wouldn't let go. For this, Stubby was officially promoted to sergeant, becoming the first dog ever to achieve rank in the US Army. During one battle, an exploding grenade peppered Stubby's body with shrapnel. At the hospital, doctors performed surgery to save the dog's life. As he slowly recovered, Stubby roamed the corridors, visiting wounded soldiers and sometimes snuggling next to them and licking their faces to bring them comfort. The grateful soldiers pinned their medals to his collar.

When Conroy and Stubby returned to the United States after the war, the famous dog hero took part in hundreds of military parades wearing a special blanket sporting dozens of war medals and badges, including an Iron Cross confiscated from that captured German spy! Stubby was permitted to stay in hotels where pets were normally not allowed. He was invited to the White House three times. He became an honorary member of the YMCA, the American Red Cross, and the American Legion.

In 1926, Stubby died peacefully in Conroy's arms. The *New York Times* published an obituary to mark the canine hero's passing. Considered a national treasure, Stubby's preserved body was put on display in Washington, DC, at the Smithsonian's National Museum of American History.

SOMETHING TO THINK ABOUT

Stubby bravely faced conflict on the battlefield. Are you facing a different sort of battle in your life? Perhaps you have a disability or disease that makes life difficult. Maybe your family life is not what it should be. Are you having trouble getting good grades in school? If so, you can ask God to help you. Ask for His help right now. You can trust God to lead you to victory.

Dear Father in heaven, I need Your help. I am not sure what to do. You know everything that troubles me. Help me to remember that everything in my life—whether it's a big problem or a small one—matters to You. I will trust You to see me through this. In Jesus's name, amen.

CHIPS

Decorated Hero of WWII

1943

Before he became the most famous American dog of World War II, Chips was just a family pet living in Pleasantville, New York. The German shepherd–collie–husky mutt was powerful and feisty. He chased the letter carrier and snapped at the garbage collector. When the US Army put out a call for canines for the Dogs of Defense program, Edward Wren and his family knew that Chips would be a good fit, so they donated him to become a guard dog.

As soon as Chips and his handler, Private John P. Rowell, finished their training, they were shipped overseas to Morocco. Chips was so good at sentry duty that he was one of the dogs used to guard the compound where President Franklin D. Roosevelt and British Prime Minister Winston Churchill met to plan an important phase of the Allied war strategy.

But it was during the Allied invasion of Sicily in Italy when Chips proved just how brave he was. The American soldiers had barely landed on the beach when they heard machine gun fire coming from a concrete hut. They quickly dropped to the ground, seeking cover. But not Chips! Growling and baring his teeth, Chips pulled away from his handler. He ran fearlessly toward the concrete hut, his long leash trailing behind him. Rowell and the other soldiers looked on with dismay. They feared their dog buddy would be killed. But the gunfire stopped. Chips grabbed one of the enemy soldiers by the neck, dragging him out of the hut. The other frightened men surrendered, their hands in the air. When the Americans inspected the hut, they discovered that Chips had yanked the machine gun off its mount.

After recovering from a scalp wound and powder burns, Chips was awarded the Purple Heart for battle wounds and the Silver Star for heroism. Press coverage of the event made Chips an overnight war hero. However, some people complained that defense dogs should not receive medals intended for soldiers. They demanded the medals be returned to the War Department.

The disappointed GIs serving with Chips held a special ceremony for their dog hero, presenting him with medals they'd made themselves. After the war, Chips was discharged from the Army and returned to his proud family in New York. On the train ride home, the celebrity dog was accompanied by reporters and photographers. A boisterous crowd eagerly awaited his arrival at the train station.

Looking back on his time spent with Chips, Rowell admitted, "We went through a lot together...he saved my life more than once when things were tough." Rowell even wrote a letter to the Wren family, saying, "I can never express in writing how I feel about him. Please take good care of him."

SOMETHING TO THINK ABOUT

God used Chips to protect Private Rowell and other American soldiers during the war. Have you experienced the Lord's protection in your life in a special way? God is always watching over us. His providential care is a wonderful thing.

Thank You, Lord, for taking care of me, even
when I'm sleeping. In Jesus's name, amen.

BELLA

A Courageous Cat

2019

Cats can be heroes too, as one Florida couple discovered when their pet, Bella, saved them from certain death. Leona and Paul Jones returned home one evening after having an early supper at a nearby restaurant. They parked their car in the garage and hurried into the house. Distracted by the pounding rain, booming thunder, and flashes of lightning, they didn't realize they'd forgotten to turn off the vehicle's engine. Later that night the couple went to bed, unaware that deadly carbon monoxide was filling the garage and drifting into their house through the ventilation system.

With her keen sense of smell, Bella detected the odor. Sensing danger, the black cat with the white tummy darted underneath the couple's bed, meowing and shrieking loudly. When the couple didn't respond, Bella yowled some more. The noise finally woke Paul and Leona. They were so weak from inhaling the poisoned air they could barely move to the phone to call 9-1-1.

Firefighters rushed to the scene and administered oxygen to the couple and to brave Bella, who was also weakened by the deadly fumes. While an ambulance rushed the couple and their cat to the hospital, emergency personnel opened the garage door and the windows in the home to allow the fumes to escape. After the life-threatening incident, Paul installed carbon monoxide detectors inside the home along with a huge sign inside the garage reminding him to turn off the car before getting out of the vehicle.

SOMETHING TO THINK ABOUT

Everyone recognized Bella's heroism. Without her devoted act, the couple would have succumbed to the poisoned air and died in their sleep.

If we are devoted to the Lord, He may use us to accomplish brave things we never dreamed we could do. And even if He doesn't, we will be happier in this life if we think of others and how we can make their day brighter or even safer. We are created in God's image. That means we share some of His personality traits. The Lord is kind and generous. We can be that way too instead of being self-absorbed or always thinking about ourselves.

Dear Lord, help us to see how we can be an encouragement to others, and then remind us to do it. In Jesus's name, amen.

TACOMA

Ready, Willing, and Able

2003

The Lord God decided to give the dolphin the best sonar ability ever devised." That's what one naval officer said regarding these amazing creatures trained by the US Navy to locate underwater mines. One of them is Tacoma, an Atlantic bottlenose dolphin, who located more than a hundred deadly explosive devices.

Dolphins can dive deeper than humans and are able to locate dangerous mines buried deep in the silt. When the water visibility is poor, Navy divers can't see the mines. They might touch the explosives, triggering them by accident. But Tacoma locates the mines using echolocation. Like sonar, this is a form of navigating by sound to detect objects in the water. A dolphin's skill is often more efficient than any of our sophisticated technology.

Tacoma is intelligent, sociable, swift, and sleek. He appears to be happy all the time because of his smiling face. He trained with Navy divers for a year in a massive tank onboard an American battleship. Then in 2003, Tacoma was transported by helicopter in a special fleece-lined traveling sleeve to a deepwater port in Iraq. He was even rubbed down with zinc ointment so he wouldn't get sunburned during the flight! In Iraq, he was released in the water to search for explosives, making sure the harbor was safe for American and British ships.

Sometimes mines detonate when there is a shift in the magnetic field caused by a ship's steel hull. Tacoma can swim near these mines without detonating them because he has no metallic body parts. He has been trained not to touch the device but to attach a recoverable buoy nearby. Navy divers then plunge into the water to neutralize the explosives. Because of Tacoma's efforts, the British ship *Sir Galahad* was able to safely deliver humanitarian aid to thousands of people in need.

SOMETHING TO THINK ABOUT

After a job well done, Tacoma receives his favorite treat—fish! Have you ever received a reward for performing a task well? Maybe you earned an A-plus on that math test you studied so hard for. Or perhaps you received a hot fudge sundae after hitting a home run for your team. Well, guess what? Eternal life is the reward for those who believe in Jesus and accept His truths in the Bible.

Thank You, Lord, for showering us with so many blessings—
right now and later on too. In Jesus's name, amen.

CAIRO

Canine SEAL Team Hero

2011

I n the predawn hours of May 2, 2011, two Black Hawk helicopters made their way to a guarded compound in Pakistan. The twenty-three members of Navy SEAL Team Six had been tasked with a top-secret mission—to capture or kill Osama bin Laden, the mastermind of the 9/11 terrorist attacks in the United States.

It had taken ten years to locate bin Laden's secret hideout. The siege was risky, and the mission was shrouded in secrecy. A highly trained Belgian Malinois named Cairo was part of the team. Cairo wore a tactical vest and "doggles"—protective eye gear for dogs. His job was to locate booby traps and detect trip wires. He'd been trained to sniff out hidden doors and false walls. He could even sniff out explosives and knew when someone was wearing a suicide vest. Cairo had been trained not to kill but to subdue anyone trying to attack the men on his team. Cairo's intimidating presence kept curious villagers from getting too close while the operation was underway. They took one look at the alert, aggressive dog and quietly left the scene.

Cairo and his handler, Will Chesney, bonded quickly during their months of exhausting combat training. Most military dogs are trained to perform one job, such as bomb detecting. Only one dog in a thousand is intelligent enough to do multiple tasks. Cairo proved to be one of the rare ones. Intelligent and driven, Cairo was unfazed by gunfire, explosions, noisy helicopter rides, and even rappelling with ropes. But at night, he liked snuggling in bed with his handler and proved to be a blanket hog! Before joining the top-secret mission, Cairo and Will served in Afghanistan, where Cairo was shot in the chest and leg while pursuing armed insurgents. Combat surgeons—not a veterinarian—provided the medical treatment that saved Cairo's life.

When the bin Laden mission was successfully accomplished, President Barak Obama presented Silver Stars to each member of the elite team. All except Cairo. The President did, however, request to meet the dog that had played a crucial role in one of America's most intense military operations. When Will Chesney retired from the Navy, he adopted Cairo and credited the dog with helping him cope with anxiety, depression, and PTSD.

SOMETHING TO THINK ABOUT

Cairo became a successful team member because of his training. Have you ever been a part of a sports team? You probably attended practice to learn the rules of the game and how to perform well. You can also train for the mission of the church—to share the good news about Jesus—by attending Bible study and worship services, learning praise songs, and helping with service projects.

God, I know You have plans for my life. Guide me into these plans. I am excited about serving You. In Jesus's name, amen.

DORY

A Dutiful Rabbit

2004

B unnies are cute and cuddly, aren't they? But can a rabbit save someone's life? Dory did. She was a giant Flemish rabbit weighing twenty pounds and standing three feet tall. She belonged to Simon and Victoria Steggall in Great Britain.

Dory had been living with them for just three months when she saved Simon's life. He had been a diabetic from his childhood, requiring several insulin shots each day. One evening, after a tiring day of work climbing up and down telephone poles, Simon settled down in his favorite chair to watch TV. That's when he lapsed into a coma. Somehow Dory sensed that the man's blood sugar levels were dangerously low. Simon was in trouble. He might die! Dory jumped into his lap. She thumped his chest and licked his face.

Puzzled by the rabbit's behavior, Victoria ordered Dory to get down. She thought her husband was simply dozing in front of the television. When she tried to rouse him, however, Victoria realized something was wrong. Grabbing Simon's glucose gel, she rubbed it on his gums. Usually, this would spike his blood-sugar levels back to normal. But this time, it didn't work. Victoria quickly called the paramedics.

At the hospital, Simon's wife told the doctor what had happened. He was quite surprised. He remarked that he'd heard of dogs and cats acting in amazing ways like this, but never a rabbit. For her life-saving deed, Dory was treated to an extra-large helping of cabbage and made an honorary animal member of the Rabbit Welfare Association.

SOMETHING TO THINK ABOUT

Dogs have been trained to respond to diabetic people's glucose levels. When a person's metabolism changes, they smell differently. People don't notice the smell, but dogs do. Dogs can be trained to recognize the odor and to warn the diabetic to take their medicine. Studies are being conducted to determine what chemical signals animals can detect and how they might be trained to be caregivers for people with special needs. But no one could explain how Dory knew that Simon was in distress. She had not been trained to detect illness. She was simply a beloved pet. Sometimes God uses animals and ordinary people to do amazing things.

Jesus's handpicked disciples were ordinary men, but the Lord empowered them to do extraordinary things in His name.

Lord, You have blessed me in so many ways. Help me to use my special gifts and talents to be a blessing to other people in my life—and to the animals too.

KERRY GOLD

Bodyguard Horse

2007

F iona Boyd and her family owned a dairy farm in Scotland. She owned a horse too—a beautiful chestnut mare named Kerry Gold. Fiona had always been a horse lover, even as a girl. She loved everything about Kerry—the way the mare nickered, how she tossed her head, the way she blew spurts of air through her nose.

One day, Fiona entered the paddock intending to remove a two-day-old calf to another pen and take its mother to the milking shed. As she prodded the little calf toward one of the farm buildings, it became frightened and began to bellow loudly. That's when the trouble began.

Usually, dairy cows are calm and mellow, but this time, the calf's mother became fiercely protective. The raging cow head-butted Fiona—hard—knocking her to the ground. When Fiona tried to get up, the cow attacked using her huge head and feet. Bleeding and in pain, Fiona tried to crawl away. But the massive cow stood over her, straddling Fiona's body, seemingly intent on crushing her. Unable to escape, Fiona curled into a ball, shielding her head with her arms. She feared she might be killed.

Then an unlikely hero came to her rescue—Kerry Gold. The

45

mare had been grazing in the same grassy paddock. She noticed Fiona huddled on the ground with the cow looming over her. Kerry seemed to sense that something was wrong. Prancing forward, Kerry charged the cow, lashing out with her rear hooves until the animal retreated. Aching and shaking, Fiona reached into the pocket of her jeans for her cell phone to call for help. Her husband took her to the emergency room. Fiona was severely bruised, and her spine was painfully twisted, but no bones were broken.

In time, Fiona made a full recovery. The Boyds lavished brave Kerry with carrots and apples. After the incident, Kerry always seemed to be at Fiona's side, acting like a bodyguard when the woman approached the cows.

SOMETHING TO THINK ABOUT

Fiona believes that when someone loves their animals, their animals will love them back. The Bible tells us in Proverbs 12:10 that godly people care for their animals and pets. Always be kind to yours. They are God's creatures too.

Thank You, Lord, for entrusting us with the care of the beloved animals You created. Sometimes they take care of us too, like Kerry Gold did by rescuing Fiona. Pets are a precious and important part of our lives. We are grateful for them. In Jesus's name, amen.

RIP

To the Rescue

1941

Not all war dogs save the lives of soldiers. During World War II, Rip—a scruffy, wirehaired mutt—displayed a talent for locating people trapped in buildings damaged by bombs. An air-raid warden named Mr. King discovered the stray wandering through the rubble-strewn streets of London, England. He tossed the remains of his sandwich to the dog, who followed him back to the station where he worked.

The dog was friendly and smart. The men in the Southill Street Air Raid Precaution Station adopted him as a mascot and named him Rip. It was during this time that London residents endured the Blitz—a nightly bombing campaign carried out by Nazi Germany's air force, called the Luftwaffe. Adolph Hitler hoped to demoralize the British people so they would surrender.

Following each bombing raid, Mr. King and the other wardens headed out to search for survivors of the air attack. Rip went with them. Despite having no training, Rip seemed to know what to do. Perhaps he thought it was some sort of game. He stood on top of smoldering rubble and sniffed the air. His nose twitched. When he detected something, he scratched the scorched bricks, barking to attract the men's attention. When Rip discovered an unconscious child buried beneath the rubble, the men quickly rescued the boy and carried him to safety.

It was dangerous work for both Rip and the men. Broken glass was everywhere. Gas leaks caused sickness. Fires often smoldered beneath the rubble. Everyone had to watch out for collapsing walls and unexploded bombs. Despite the dangers, Rip rescued more than a hundred trapped victims. He became the first civil defense search-and-rescue dog ever. Although he had no official training, his success impressed war officials, who started a training center to teach other dogs how to help air raid wardens too. After the war, Rip was awarded the Dicken medal by the People's Dispensary for Sick Animals. He wore this on his collar until the day he died in 1946. His tombstone reads, "We also serve—for the dog whose body lies here played his part in the Battle of Britain."

SOMETHING TO THINK ABOUT

Did you know that a dog's wet nose has three hundred million smell detectors? Our human nose has only six million. A dog can detect a teaspoon of sugar diluted in a million gallons of water. That's about the same amount of water it takes to fill two Olympic-size swimming pools! Rip used the amazing gift God gave him to bravely rescue people trapped beneath the rubble.

What can you learn from Rip's life? What gifts has God given you so that you might serve others too?

Heavenly Father, help me to embrace my uniqueness. Show me how to use my skills and my natural talents for Your glory and purpose, just as Rip did. In Jesus's name, amen.

NINGNONG

On Alert

2004

Wouldn't it be fun to be friends with an elephant? While vacationing for a month in Thailand with her parents, eight-year-old Amber Mason of Great Britain made friends with a young elephant named Ningnong. Each morning Amber ran down to the beach to give a banana to her pachyderm pal. Ningnong's handler allowed Amber and other tourists to ride the elephant along the shore. Soon Ningnong began to watch for Amber. Sometimes he tickled her neck with his trunk. They became good buddies.

On the day after Christmas, the tide was unusually low. Stranded fish flopped all over the beach. Ningnong's handler began picking up the fish for his lunch. Soon other people came down to the shore with baskets to collect fish too. But Ningnong acted nervous. He didn't want to walk along the beach. Instead, the young elephant began running toward the hotel with Amber on his back. Then came the devastating tsunami—a massive wall of water caused by a powerful 9.3 magnitude earthquake on the ocean floor. The one-hundred-foot wave slammed onto shore. Ningnong braced himself against the powerful surge of water. Amber hung on tight.

Alerted to the danger by people screaming, Amber's panicked parents abandoned their breakfast and raced outside the hotel. Where's the elephant, they wondered? They knew wherever they found Ningnong, Amber would be with him. Searching frantically, the Masons discovered Ningnong seeking shelter beside a high wall, their daughter still clinging to his back. The relieved family managed to race upstairs to their hotel room before the second powerful wave hit, washing away several rooms below theirs and everything in them.

Tens of thousands of people died that day throughout Asia. But not Amber. She told reporters how the alert young elephant had saved her life. Amber's grateful mother promised to send money each month to the handler for Ningnong's care. Oddly enough, following the deadly tsunami, people reported that other elephants besides Ningnong had sensed the danger. Early that morning, the elephants roared noisily, breaking their chains to run toward high ground. Other animals, such as monkeys, flamingos, dogs, and antelopes were seen fleeing the coastline and heading for the hills. Could they feel the shock waves from the earthquake or the low-frequency vibrations from the oncoming waves? No one really knows.

SOMETHING TO THINK ABOUT

There are many Proverbs in the Old Testament concerning friendship. Proverbs 17:17 reminds us that "a friend loves [or cares] at all times." Proverbs 27:9 points out that "the sweet smell of perfume and oils is pleasant, and so is good advice from a friend" (NCV). Ningnong proved to be a true friend as he carried young Amber to safety rather than bucking her off when he fled from the tsunami. What kind of friend are you?

Lord, help me to be a caring and trustworthy
friend. I ask it in Jesus's name, amen.

CHER AMI

Brave Pigeon of World War I

1918

I f you've ever seen pigeons in the park, you may wonder how birds could be helpful in wartime. The use of messenger pigeons in war and in peace goes back many centuries—the Romans, Persians, and Mongols. During World War I, American and British troops relied heavily on carrier pigeons, especially when radios and telegraph wires were destroyed. Birds were faster than messenger dogs and harder to shoot than dispatch riders on bicycles. Although pigeons generally didn't like flying in fog or rain, they usually performed their important task anyway. After the war, many veteran soldiers and pilots gave credit where credit was due, saying, "I'm standing here today because of a pigeon."

Cher Ami, a blue checkered pigeon, was the most famous American bird of the First World War. She carried messages inside a tiny tube tied to her leg. She successfully delivered more than a dozen messages during battles in France, usually covering twenty-five miles in eighteen minutes. Her most famous mission, in which she nearly died, was in October 1918.

When a desperate American platoon of five hundred men—most of them from New York—became pinned down by Germans, they used pigeons to call for help: "MANY WOUNDED.

WE CANNOT ESCAPE." The first bird was killed by enemy fire. The soldiers tried again: "MEN ARE SUFFERING. CAN SUPPORT NOT BE SENT?" The second pigeon was shot down too. Cher Ami became their last hope of survival. She took to the bullet-filled skies but was immediately shot down. The soldiers despaired. Then something amazing happened. Cher Ami struggled to her feet, shook her feathers, and took to the skies again. She traveled twenty-five miles in less than half an hour to deliver the important message to Allied headquarters. When she landed in the pigeon loft, handlers discovered a bullet lodged in her small chest. One thin leg dangled by a tendon. Cher Ami received immediate medical care, and the remaining two hundred war-weary soldiers were rescued.

Back in the United States at Fort Monmouth, New Jersey, Cher Ami was fitted with a small wooden leg and retired from service. Even today her heroism is not forgotten. In 2019, she became one of the first creatures to receive a Medal of Bravery from Animals in War & Peace.

SOMETHING TO THINK ABOUT

The name Cher Ami means "dear friend" in French. Jesus said, "Greater love has no one than this: to lay down one's life for one's friends" (John 15:13). Jesus is the greatest friend of all!

Dear Jesus, thank You for being our friend. Help me to trust You more each day. In Your name I ask it. Amen.

DORSEY

The Mail Dog

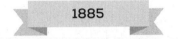

1885

When postmaster Everett Stacy first set eyes on the black-and-white border collie he dubbed Dorsey, he never imagined that one day the shaggy stray would become a national celebrity.

Three times a week a stagecoach delivered mail to the silver mining town of Calico, California. Stacy's responsibilities included sorting the mail and delivering letters addressed to miners in Bismarck, a nearby mining camp. Dorsey accompanied Stacy on his rounds over the rugged mountain terrain. He became used to the routine and the mile and a half route.

One day, Stacy was unable to make the trip. He attached the mail pouch to Dorsey's back, urging the dog to head for Bismarck. Dorsey hesitated at first, perhaps reluctant to go on his own. Finally, after a little persuasion, the dog scampered down the familiar trail. Dorsey returned the next day with outgoing letters tucked in the pouch.

Soon Dorsey was making deliveries all by himself. Stacy devised homemade leather booties to protect Dorsey's tender feet from sharp rocks and blistering sand along the steep, rugged trail. The delighted miners treated Dorsey to steak dinners upon his arrival.

Everyone petted and praised him. Letters were unloaded from the pouch and outgoing mail put in. News about Dorsey, along with his photograph, appeared in newspapers across the nation. Readers enjoyed learning about the clever dog-delivery system. When the mine closed, one of the owners took Dorsey to live with him in San Francisco, where the famous dog lived out his remaining years in a mansion.

SOMETHING TO THINK ABOUT

Have you ever felt like Dorsey—nervous or hesitant to do something on your own? Most everyone feels that way sometimes. But we needn't feel afraid. Jesus is standing right beside us! Here's a good Bible verse to memorize: "Be strong and courageous. Do not be afraid; do not be discouraged, for the LORD your God will be with you wherever you go" (Joshua 1:9).

Heavenly Father, sometimes I feel afraid, but I know You are with me. Please touch me with Your reassuring peace. In Jesus's name, amen.

ANDY

The Gutsy Goose

1989

ndy was born without feet. Instead, the little gray goose had two calloused knobs. Andy could barely stand upright on his twiglike legs. When he tried to walk, he'd lurch forward onto his chest. But Andy had pluck. Every time he fell, Andy pulled himself up again. When Gene Fleming noticed the gutsy goose staggering around his sister-in-law's Nebraska farm, he felt sorry for him. Gene made up his mind to help.

At first, Gene considered making a small skateboard for Andy to zip around on. He changed his mind and bought a pair of shoes instead—white leather baby shoes, size 0. He stuffed the shoes with rubber sponge. He poked holes in them so water could drain out. Picking up the goose, Gene smoothed Andy's feathers and slipped on the shoes. He tied the laces. Using a harness and a leash, Gene spent hours coaxing Andy to walk. When Andy got the hang of it, Gene unhooked the leash. The little goose with the black shoe-button eyes toddled everywhere. He even swam happily in the pond. He honked with joy. When the white baby shoes wore out, Gene bought Andy a pair of little red sneakers.

Most geese are snappish, but not Andy. He liked people and people liked him. Word about Andy spread. He and Gene were invited everywhere. Wearing his little tennis shoes and a special harness and leash, Andy visited libraries and schools, honking hello as he waddled in. Gene reminded the audience that sometimes a little help can make a big difference, that they should keep their eyes open to see how they might be able to assist a person or animal in need. Both Gene and Andy inspired children to do their best, especially those youngsters with disabilities. Andy became a national hero when an article about him appeared in *People* magazine.

SOMETHING TO THINK ABOUT

Gene's compassion and Andy's persistence led to success. Neither of them gave up. They kept trying. There's an old saying that goes, "If at first you don't succeed, try, try again." You, too, can be successful if you always remember that faith in God is your greatest asset. Those who let God accomplish amazing things through them do so because they believe He can. Jesus reminds us, "With God all things are possible" (Matthew 19:26).

Lord, thank You for people like Gene, who showed compassion to a helpless little goose. I want to be a caring and compassionate person too. In Jesus's name, amen.

COW 569

Life Saver

2004

ew Zealand dairy farmer Kim Riley almost drowned when the Manawatu River overflowed its banks during a torrential rainstorm. Thankfully, she didn't drown. She was saved by a cow! Yes, really—a cow. Hundreds of people moved to higher ground during the flood, but not Kim's family. They stayed to ride out the disaster and hoped for the best. The Rileys owned 900 cows—too many to name, so each animal wore a numbered ear tag. Cow 569, a black-and-white Friesian, wasn't much to look at. She had a funny face and a bent ear, but she proved to be very special.

It was still dark at 4:00 a.m. on that fateful morning when Kim went outside to guide the cows from the pasture to the milking shed. She was shocked by what she saw. Because of the flooding, some of the cows stood knee-deep in mud. Others floated in the warm, smelly floodwaters. Kim wondered how she would be able to get them all to the shed. Suddenly, the surging river swept Kim off her feet. Her rubber boots, leggings, and coat filled with water. She struggled to rip off her gear. Cows surrounded her, mooing in distress. Some of the animals swam right over the top of her. Bruised and bumped, Kim tried to reach solid ground.

She struggled against the flooding and the tumble of cows for nearly an hour. She became weary and had no way to call for help.

That's when Cow 569 peeled off from the herd, dog-paddling straight toward Kim. Most people don't realize that cows are good swimmers, but they really are. Huffing and snorting, Cow 569 swam in front of Kim, allowing the woman to lurch forward to grab on to her neck. Kim hung on tight. The wet, warm cow—smelling of grass and mud—paddled toward a hill with Kim clinging to her side. When they reached firm ground, Kim let go of the animal's neck and gave the cow a grateful pat of thanks.

Although she couldn't explain how or why it happened, Kim realized that the buoyant bovine with the funny face and bent ear had saved her life. Cow 569 became a media sensation with her photo in all the newspapers. Later, Kim wrote a children's picture book memorializing her cow's heroism. Because Cow 569 proved to be so special, the Rileys gave her a new ear tag that read "Lifesaver."

SOMETHING TO THINK ABOUT

Like Cow 569, you're special too. Jesus told His followers, "Don't be afraid; you are more valuable to God than a whole flock of sparrows" (Luke 12:7 NLT). Or a whole herd of cows!

Thank You, Creator God, for loving me and always watching over me. I know I am special in Your eyes—more special than cows and sparrows. Please help me to remember that always.

IGLOO

Eager Explorer

1930

gloo is the only dog to have explored both the North and South Poles. The short-haired fox terrier was the constant companion of Admiral Richard E. Byrd—best known for being the first man to fly over both Poles. After their successful Arctic voyage to the north, Byrd sailed south to Antarctica in 1928, intent on flying over the South Pole too. This expedition was considered so dangerous that newspaper reporters prepared the men's obituaries ahead of time, certain many would die.

Igloo loved life aboard the ship despite the slippery decks, rough seas, and danger of frostbite. This time, dozens of Eskimo sled dogs were chained onboard, and they lunged at the spunky terrier. Igloo soon taught them who was boss. When the men established Little America in Antarctica, he protected the camp from curious Adélie penguins, occasionally receiving a *whomp* from a flipper for his efforts.

The crew had warm, custom-made clothing for the expedition. Even Igloo was outfitted with camel-hair trousers, a matching coat, and lace-up boots to protect his feet from the ice. At first, Igloo didn't like his new outfit. He pouted, refusing to go outside wearing his clothes. But soon he relented. He even pulled the coat out of his fur-lined bed and dropped it at Byrd's feet when he was eager for a walk.

Following the Antarctica expedition, Byrd was hailed as an international hero. So was Igloo. Together they attended banquets and parades. Igloo even received his own gold medal. He sometimes acted shy, hiding underneath the banquet table. Byrd could always coax him out again with a bit of cake. When Igloo died, a heartbroken Byrd buried him with this gravestone inscription: "He was more than just a friend." Byrd refused to adopt another dog.

SOMETHING TO THINK ABOUT

Byrd once said, "Igloo ... opened my eyes to the fact that animals can think and suffer, be loyal and gallant." Have you ever thought of an animal being gallant? The word means being courteously firm or consistent in allegiance to someone or to a cause. It can also mean being brave and heroic. Igloo was all those things. He was spunky and adventurous too.

Do you ever feel that God is leading you into an exciting adventure? Will you follow God's leading? If you do, you'll have the satisfaction of knowing you've been faithful to the Lord's will for your life.

Heavenly Father, where You lead me, I will follow. In Jesus's name, amen.

TOMMY

Trained for an Emergency

2006

It started out as an ordinary day for Gary Rosheisen of Columbus, Ohio—until he fell out of bed onto the floor next to his wheelchair. In pain and weak from chronic illness, Gary couldn't pull himself up to reach the emergency cord. Nor was he wearing his medical alert necklace, so he couldn't notify paramedics that he needed help. He did the only thing he could do—he called out to his cat, Tommy.

Gary had rescued the orange-and-tan tabby from a shelter three years prior to this accident. He looked forward to having a pet for companionship. Gary lived by himself and often felt lonely. He hoped Tommy would bring some joy into his life and help lower his stress level. Because he'd suffered several ministrokes in the past, Gary taught Tommy to call 9-1-1 on speed dial in case of an emergency. He kept the telephone on the floor so the cat could reach it when necessary. Together Gary and Tommy repeated the drill over and over again. But was the cat really catching on? Had the training been successful? Gary found out on the day of his accident.

Tommy did indeed press the right button with his paw. Concerned when no one responded vocally, the emergency dispatcher sent police officers to the scene to investigate. They found Tommy lying on the floor next to the phone, and Gary immobilized beside his wheelchair. Tommy's quick response saved Gary's life. Tommy had taken good care of the man who took care of him.

SOMETHING TO THINK ABOUT

Cats sometimes have the reputation of being aloof—that means not friendly or playful like dogs. Some say cats are not as devoted to their owners as dogs are. But Tommy proved that love and loyalty are not limited to any one kind of creature.

You can be loving and loyal to your family members too. Do you know how to call 9-1-1 in case of an emergency in your home? That would be a good thing to learn today.

Dear heavenly Father, help me to be especially kind to members of my family and to show them gratitude for their love for me. I want to focus on what's right in my life and not so much on the disappointments. In Jesus's name, amen.

TOMMY

Trained for an Emergency

2006

It started out as an ordinary day for Gary Rosheisen of Columbus, Ohio—until he fell out of bed onto the floor next to his wheelchair. In pain and weak from chronic illness, Gary couldn't pull himself up to reach the emergency cord. Nor was he wearing his medical alert necklace, so he couldn't notify paramedics that he needed help. He did the only thing he could do—he called out to his cat, Tommy.

Gary had rescued the orange-and-tan tabby from a shelter three years prior to this accident. He looked forward to having a pet for companionship. Gary lived by himself and often felt lonely. He hoped Tommy would bring some joy into his life and help lower his stress level. Because he'd suffered several ministrokes in the past, Gary taught Tommy to call 9-1-1 on speed dial in case of an emergency. He kept the telephone on the floor so the cat could reach it when necessary. Together Gary and Tommy repeated the drill over and over again. But was the cat really catching on? Had the training been successful? Gary found out on the day of his accident.

Tommy did indeed press the right button with his paw. Concerned when no one responded vocally, the emergency dispatcher sent police officers to the scene to investigate. They found Tommy lying on the floor next to the phone, and Gary immobilized beside his wheelchair. Tommy's quick response saved Gary's life. Tommy had taken good care of the man who took care of him.

SOMETHING TO THINK ABOUT

Cats sometimes have the reputation of being aloof—that means not friendly or playful like dogs. Some say cats are not as devoted to their owners as dogs are. But Tommy proved that love and loyalty are not limited to any one kind of creature.

You can be loving and loyal to your family members too. Do you know how to call 9-1-1 in case of an emergency in your home? That would be a good thing to learn today.

Dear heavenly Father, help me to be especially kind to members of my family and to show them gratitude for their love for me. I want to focus on what's right in my life and not so much on the disappointments. In Jesus's name, amen.

MURPHY

A Daring Donkey

1915

Have you ever heard the expression "strong as an ox"? "Fast as a cheetah"? What about "brave as a donkey"? Probably not. Donkeys aren't usually considered courageous creatures. But during World War I, a small gray donkey named Murphy earned the respect of Australian and New Zealand Army Corps (ANZAC) troops fighting in Gallipoli, Turkey. Murphy was part of a donkey ambulance that carried wounded soldiers from the battlefield to the field hospital on the beach, where they could be evacuated to safety. At first, stretcher bearer John Simpson carried wounded men from the firing line back to the beach over his shoulders. Then, noticing a small gray donkey being used to carry supplies, Simpson snatched Murphy's bridle and decided to put him to work evacuating the wounded.

Together Simpson and Murphy made endless trips over the craggy hills amid falling bombs and sniper bullets to rescue hundreds of wounded men. Both Murphy and Simpson drove themselves to exhaustion. Their pluck gained legendary status among the weary troops.

Gallipoli was a terrible place for men and animals. The heat was unbearable in the summer and the cold bitter in the winter. The noise of gunfire was constant. There was a water shortage, and the men had nothing to eat but rock-hard biscuits and canned meat.

During the heat of battle, weary soldiers asked, "Has the bloke with the donk stopped yet?" But Murphy and Simpson didn't stop. They kept going. In twenty-four days, they rescued three hundred soldiers, earning the admiration of the fighting men. Sadly, Simpson was eventually killed by enemy machine gun fire. He was only twenty-two years old. But Murphy survived the war. The grateful ANZAC troops now saw the humble creature with new eyes and did all they could to make sure the brave little donkey was returned to his home in Greece. They respected his pluck. Many years later, Murphy was honored with a Purple Cross, the highest award for an animal from the Royal Society for Prevention of Cruelty to Animals.

SOMETHING TO THINK ABOUT

Many years after the Battle of Gallipoli, tens of thousands of mules were used during World War II. Did you know that a mule is part donkey and part horse? Mules ate less than horses and were more sure-footed. Hardy and resilient, these animals carried ammo and supplies along winding mountain passes in Burma. They were dropped by parachute into the jungles of China to serve with General Chiang Kai-shek's Allied forces. Because their noisy braying might alert Japanese troops, more than five thousand mules had their vocal cords cut by army vets under general anesthesia.

When the Allies landed in Italy in 1943, they bought thousands of mules to help transport weapons and supplies through the rugged mountain terrain. The animals were shipped in from Iran and Persia. American officers, fearing the mules' gray coats would be noticeable by the enemy, insisted that every mule be dyed brown! During the winter months, the animals were allowed to go back to their natural gray color, which blended in with the snow.

Dear Lord, help me to appreciate just how special
we all are. Murphy was not "just a donkey." Let
me see someone with new eyes today.

NORMAN

Brave and Blind

1996

Norman, a yellow Labrador retriever, was scheduled to be euthanized—until Annette MacDonald adopted him from a shelter. She liked the friendly dog immediately, and he liked her too. Soon after she brought him home, however, Annette realized something was wrong. Norman kept bumping into things. A visit to the veterinarian confirmed her fears: Norman was going blind, and it was incurable. Annette vowed to love darling Norman even more.

She and her husband, Steve, lived along the Necanicum River in Oregon, where Norman enjoyed strolling along the beach. But one day, after Annette let him off his leash, Norman dashed down the shore with amazing speed. Worried Norman might injure himself, Annette tried to catch up. Norman had never run away before. What was going on? What Annette didn't know was that a fourteen-year-old girl named Lisa Nibley was drowning in a dangerous undertow. Norman had heard the teenager's cries for help above the roar of the waves.

Amazed, Annette watched as Norman plunged courageously into the water, paddling out toward the drowning girl. Frightened and exhausted, Lisa tried to grab hold of Norman's collar, but her arms were shaking from fatigue, and she couldn't hold on. Norman came back to try again. This time Lisa got a firm grip, and the dog towed Lisa to shore. Astonished, Annette wondered how Norman knew what to do. He'd never been trained to perform such a rescue. And why had he dashed to the aid of a complete stranger? She couldn't explain it.

Safely on shore, Lisa clung to Annette, sobbing her thanks to the woman and dog who'd saved her life. Lisa admitted praying to God for help. God answered her prayer. Lisa insisted that Norman and Annette were guardian angels sent to her rescue. Brave Norman was hailed as a hero and featured in the Hero Pets issue of *People* Magazine.

SOMETHING TO THINK ABOUT

Following Lisa's miraculous rescue, her family offered to pay for an operation to restore Norman's sight. However, the dog's condition could not be cured through surgery. Despite his permanent blindness, Norman led a full and happy life. Many blind people do the same. There are numerous resources to assist them.

Have you heard of Helen Keller? She was the most famous blind person of the twentieth century. She was also deaf, but her disabilities didn't prevent her from earning a college education and becoming a bestselling author.

Before Helen, a little girl named Laura Bridgman, who could not see, hear, or speak, learned to read and communicate at the Perkins Institute in Massachusetts in 1839. She was the first blind, deaf, and mute person to receive an education.

Dear Lord, please give me a steadfast faith that keeps me in a trusting relationship with You, even in the middle of my problems. With You, there are no hopeless circumstances. In Jesus's name, amen.

WILLIE

The Watchful Parrot

2009

Have you ever thought about words being so powerful they can actually save someone's life? Willie, a green and gray Quaker parrot, is credited with saving the life of a choking two-year-old toddler when he frantically flapped his wings and squawked out the words, "Mama, baby" to alert his owner to the emergency. Nineteen-year-old Megan Howard darted into the kitchen just as little Hannah Kuusk, the child she was babysitting, turned blue in the face. Her lips turned blue too. With her heart pounding, Megan quickly performed the Heimlich maneuver by applying pressure to the child's abdomen, which dislodged the piece of Pop-Tart stuck in her windpipe.

Megan credited her quick-thinking pet with saving Hannah's life. Willie routinely called his owner Mama, but he astonished Megan by adding the word "baby" as he shrieked his alarm. He'd never spoken that word before! Willie was honored by the Denver chapter of the American Red Cross at their Breakfast of Champions, where he received the Animal Lifesaver Award. The governor of Colorado and the mayor of Denver attended the ceremony to congratulate the feathered hero.

So what is a Quaker parrot? These birds appear to quake or

quiver when they are excited or irritated. Baby Quaker parrots shake all over when they beg for food. Sometimes called monk parakeets, quaker parrots are known to live for twenty or thirty years. They are real chatterboxes that speak clearly and are easily understood.

SOMETHING TO THINK ABOUT

Like most parrots, Willie had a varied vocabulary. He could say "come here" and "give me a kiss." He could also imitate a cat, dog, and chicken. When Willie gave the warning that saved the little girl's life, he acted with clear intention. The timing of his squawking and his word choice were more than mere coincidence. He used the words appropriately to signal an emergency. Was Willie simply responding to the child's apparent distress? Or did he truly care for Hannah and realize she needed help? No one knows for sure. Hannah's mother believes that animals are far more intelligent than we give them credit for.

Our words may also influence someone else to take action. Speaking up might even save someone's life.

Lord in heaven, please use my words for Your purposes
as you did with Willie. May my words always
be kind and true. And let me be quick to praise
and slow to grumble. In Jesus's name, amen.

SMOKY

Brave and Devoted

1944

Known as "the angel in the foxhole," Smoky became a tremendous morale booster for American troops fighting in the jungles of the Pacific during World War II. Corporal William Wynne discovered the hungry little Yorkshire terrier on the side of a dirt road. He named her for the color of her fur. Smoky was no taller than his combat boot. She fit neatly inside Wynne's combat helmet. The pair became inseparable. They shared C-rations, SPAM, and dehydrated eggs. Wynne even shared his military-issue vitamins with the mini mutt, who never became ill throughout the war. Together they survived a typhoon on Okinawa, dozens of air raids in New Guinea, and twelve combat missions throughout the Pacific islands.

The pint-sized pup was so smart that Wynne trained her to do all sorts of tricks. She could spell her name with wooden alphabet blocks and walk a tightrope blindfolded. Wynne even made her a tiny scooter. The delighted troops never tired of watching Smoky scoot around the barracks. Smoky even saved Wynne's life onboard ship one day as they sailed to the Philippines—she alerted him to an incoming bomb from an enemy plane. They safely ducked for cover, but the eight men standing nearby were killed.

When it came to installing an important communication cable on an American airbase on Luzon Island in the Philippines, Smoky again proved her worth. Normally, the three-day task would have involved moving 40 aircraft and 250 men off the base, exposing them to enemy attack. The sergeant in charge had a better idea. He suggested tying a string around Smoky's collar and having her crawl through a narrow pipe in the dark, threading the lines behind her. Wynne knew it would be a tight squeeze for his delicate little dog, so he agreed on one condition: If Smoky became stuck, they would dig her out immediately. The sergeant agreed. Coaxed by Wynne's voice at the other end of the long pipe, Smoky bravely completed the task. Her efforts were believed to have saved the lives of the men and prevented the aircraft from being bombed by the enemy. As a reward she was treated to a juicy steak dinner—the meat cut into tiny bits appropriate for her small size.

When Wynne was hospitalized with a mosquito-borne disease known as dengue fever, the doctor allowed the pup to sleep in Wynne's bed. She was a huge hit with the nurses and other medical personnel. They carried her through the wards, where she entertained sick soldiers with her variety of tricks. When the US Army held a contest to identify the best military mascot, it came as no surprise that Smoky was named champion of the Southwest Pacific area.

After the war, Wynne returned to Ohio with his tiny terrier. Smoky received a hero's welcome, her photograph appearing in various newspapers. Requests for interviews came pouring in as did requests for Smoky to visit the sick and injured in area hospitals. Not long after his return, Wynne married his high school sweetheart, Margie. When they headed out on their honeymoon road trip, guess who went with them? Smoky, of course!

SOMETHING TO THINK ABOUT

After the war, Smoky received the Certificate for Animal Bravery and Devotion from the People's Dispensary for Sick Animals. Today there are numerous monuments dedicated to this brave mini mutt.

Sometimes God chooses seemingly insignificant animals and people to perform significant tasks. Remember, David was a teenage shepherd boy when God chose him to become the next king of Israel after Saul. And Mary was just a girl when God selected her to become the mother of His one and only Son, Jesus. What do you think the Lord is preparing you to do for His kingdom? Perhaps He will use you now and not wait until you reach adulthood.

Heavenly Father, give me the courage to serve You at any time, in any place. In Jesus's name, amen.

LULU

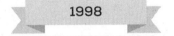

Lifesaving Pig

1998

"Help! Help me!" Jo Ann Altsman cried in a loud voice. Suffering from a heart attack, she had collapsed to the floor and couldn't reach her phone. Jo Ann was alone in her Pennsylvania home—her husband was out fishing. There was no one to hear her cries for help except LuLu, the family's 150-pound Vietnamese pot-bellied pig.

LuLu sobbed noisily and tried to kiss Jo Ann, who had tears streaming down her face. Aware of the woman's distress, the pig squeezed through the too-small doggie door and pushed open the outside gate, cutting her stomach as she did so. Running out to the street, LuLu plunked down in the road and played dead, forcing cars to move slowly around her. Finally, a passing motorist stopped to see if the pig was injured. That's when LuLu scrambled to her feet and waddled back to the house, whimpering and snorting all the way.

The man, noting the abrasions on LuLu's stomach, followed. Hearing Jo Ann's feeble cries for help, he quickly called 9-1-1. When the ambulance arrived, LuLu tried to go along for the ride, but the medics shooed her away. At the hospital, Jo Ann underwent emergency surgery. The doctor told her that LuLu's amazing actions had helped to save her life. Grateful, Jo Ann rewarded LuLu with a jelly donut when she was released from the hospital.

Soon LuLu became a media celebrity. The American Society for the Prevention of Cruelty to Animals hosted a fancy award luncheon for the piggy hero, who munched peanuts while guests lavished her with praise. Everyone marveled at LuLu's intelligence and her loving concern for Jo Ann. LuLu passed away in 2003, but the Altsman family never forgot her bravery.

SOMETHING TO THINK ABOUT

Interestingly, at the time of her medical emergency, Jo Ann also had a dog—an American Eskimo named Bear. The dog barked noisily in response to Jo Ann's cries for help, but he did nothing else. Bear didn't try to comfort Jo Ann or go for help like LuLu did. That's one reason people marveled at the pig's remarkable behavior. What caused LuLu to react as she did? Was she smarter than Bear? Did she love Jo Ann more deeply?

Some scientists and farmers insist that pigs are smarter than dogs, that pigs may actually be the smartest of all domesticated animals! Could that possibly be true? Who knows? God created many wonderful creatures—some more extraordinary than others. We should treat all animals with kindness because the Lord has made us responsible for this beautiful world in which we live—and all the creatures who live in it with us.

Dear heavenly Father, open my eyes to the goodness around me. Help me to appreciate the special people and special animals You bring into my life. In Jesus's name, amen.

SEAMAN

Courageous Companion

1804–1806

He was a strong swimmer, capable hunter, and vigilant watchdog. His owner, Captain Meriwether Lewis, paid $20 for the Newfoundland—a large amount of money in those days. He named him Seaman in keeping with the tradition of giving dogs of this breed a nautical name. Lewis's four-footed companion proved his worth many times during the two-year wilderness journey known as the Lewis and Clark Expedition. This was the first overland journey to the Pacific coast and back. President Thomas Jefferson commissioned the Corps of Discovery in 1803 to explore the Louisiana Purchase and the land near the Pacific Ocean. He wanted Lewis, Captain William Clark, and the men under their command to make maps and take notes about the natives, the wildlife, and the plants.

It was sometimes difficult to provide enough food for forty hungry men on the move. Seaman proved helpful by catching wild ducks and geese. He was good at catching squirrels too. Lewis recorded in his diary that these were quite tasty when fried. Seaman patrolled the camp perimeter at night, keeping away grizzlies and mountain lions. Like his human companions, Seaman also endured bad weather, troublesome thorns, and annoying mosquitos.

On one occasion, the dog got in a fight with a beaver. Seaman's leg bled heavily, but Lewis's medical attention saved the dog's life. Seaman returned the favor when he saved Lewis and Clark from being trampled to death by a raging buffalo. The huge animal dashed straight for their teepee. When Seaman barked ferociously and charged the buffalo, it veered away. Had the beast smashed into the teepee where the explorers were sleeping, the two men would have been severely injured or even killed. After chasing the buffalo away from camp, Seaman returned panting and out of breath. He then lay down in front of Lewis's teepee as though nothing exciting had happened.

Seaman made friends with teenaged Sacagawea, the group's Shoshone guide and wife of Toussaint Charbonneau, the French-Canadian interpreter. When the girl and dog approached a village for the first time, the natives marveled at Seaman's size and obvious strength. They'd never seen a dog like this before. The friendly arrival of Sacagawea and Seaman ahead of the men assured the natives that their visit would be a peaceful one.

SOMETHING TO THINK ABOUT

Because of Seaman's vigilance, the expedition was never attacked by a bear. Some historians consider this to be rather amazing because of the number of grizzlies and black bears roaming the West at that time.

One who is vigilant keeps careful watch for possible danger or difficulties. The apostle Peter warned Christians to "be sober, be vigilant; because your adversary the devil walks about like a roaring lion, seeking whom he may devour" (1 Peter 5:8 NKJV). Satan is always looking for ways to make us stumble and fall away from trusting the Lord. How might God use you to be vigilant?

Dear Lord, please keep us safe when we travel. The streets are busy, and sometimes the trip is long, like the Lewis and Clark expedition. Help us reach our destination safely. In Jesus's name, amen.

FONZIE

The Devoted Dolphin

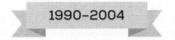

1990–2004

A 600-pound Atlantic bottlenose dolphin swam around a lagoon at a research center in Florida. Fonzie noticed a boy slumped in his mother's lap on the platform's edge. Fonzie swam near, staring at the boy and sensing something was wrong. Fonzie was right. Three-year-old Joe Hoagland had just endured his third open-heart surgery, during which he'd suffered a stroke. He couldn't stand, walk, or hold up his head. Doctors told his parents that Joe would never improve. They predicted he'd constantly need special care, requiring a wheelchair for the rest of his life.

Fonzie swam around the lagoon again, trying to get Joe's attention. Something happened then that changed Joe's life forever—and Fonzie's too. The dolphin splashed him—right in the face! Joe giggled. A special friendship was born that day.

Mrs. Hoagland cried for joy. It had been a long time since she'd seen her little boy smiling. She took Joe to the center every morning. Wearing a life vest, Joe bobbed in the water, watching the dolphins. Fonzie kept the other dolphins away. He gently nuzzled Joe's left side. It was immobile, useless. Fonzie seemed to sense something was wrong with that side of Joe's small body.

He let Joe grab his dorsal fin with his right hand while slowly swimming around the lagoon.

Therapists told Joe he could feed Fonzie a fish but only if he used his left hand. Joe exercised his left hand and arm until he was strong enough. Soon he could hold a hoop for Fonzie to jump through.

As the years passed, Joe began swimming on his own. He could walk too, carrying a bucket of fish to Fonzie. The dramatic change stunned everyone.

Joe's grateful parents founded a special program called Island Dolphin Care so that children with heart disease, autism, cancer, cerebral palsy, and other conditions could enjoy the same kind of therapy that provided seemingly miraculous results for Joe. When Joe grew up, he joined the research center team. He and Fonzie helped other children with disabilities. Fonzie was the first dolphin to demonstrate the life-changing benefits of dolphin-assisted therapy.

Fonzie has passed away, but new dolphins have joined the center and help to provide the amazing therapy that gives youngsters hope and healing.

SOMETHING TO THINK ABOUT

Perhaps you will grow up to be like Joe and Fonzie, helping children or adults overcome their disabilities. Or maybe you'll become a physical therapist who helps athletes and other people recover from their injuries. Even now, when you help someone at school or lend a hand around the house, you feel good about it, don't you? The Lord can use any person or any creature to accomplish His purpose. And that includes you!

Thank You, Lord, for caring about us and for sending us help when we need it the most. In Jesus's name, amen.

STORMY

Stouthearted Mare

2010

When an elderly brown quarter horse was found wandering the woods in Louisiana and surviving on tree bark, local authorities captured the starving mare and handed her over to a local rescue organization. Volunteers dubbed her Stormy and soon restored her health. She knew how to wear a saddle and carry a rider. She could jog with cadence and style. Stormy proved to be a calm, easygoing mare—just the kind Kevin and Kathy Leonard wanted for their nine-year-old daughter. Emma adored Stormy. She rode Stormy every day after finishing her homework and chores. She lovingly painted the mare's hooves with hot-pink nail polish.

Then one September afternoon, Emma went riding bareback toward the woods near her home. Her seven-year-old brother, Liam, skipped along beside her carrying his rubber-band gun, pretending to be a foot soldier scouting for enemies. As they neared the woods, Stormy became skittish. She snuffled noisily and became almost too frisky for Emma to control. Suddenly, a wild boar crashed through the underbrush, snorting menacingly. It had huge, scary-looking tusks and long brown bristles. Emma screamed for her little brother to run, but Liam froze with fear.

As the boar advanced toward them, Stormy went into action. First, she positioned herself between the boar and the little boy. Using her muzzle, Stormy nudged Liam back toward the house. Then, with Emma clinging tightly to her neck, Stormy kicked the boar with her rear hooves. Squealing with pain, the wild pig bolted for the woods. Emma and Liam were safe! They returned home crying with relief and babbling to their mother about what had happened.

Mrs. Leonard was amazed. Most horses would have fled from the dangerous situation. It's the natural thing to do. But Stormy, for whatever reason, bravely chose to protect Emma and Liam in the only way she knew how. Mrs. Leonard believed the mare was motivated by love.

SOMETHING TO THINK ABOUT

The Leonard family was grateful for Stormy's unexpected equine valor. Animals and people have a survival instinct when their lives are in danger—an urge to run away. Heroism is sometimes described as overcoming that survival instinct in order to save someone else.

We can't help every person or animal in distress, but like Stormy, we can be ready to help when the Lord prompts us to do so.

Lord, when I feel afraid or uncertain, help
me trust in You! In Jesus's name, amen.

BARRY

The Bravest Saint Bernard

1812

Have you heard of Switzerland's national dog? His name is Barry der Menschenretter—a big name for a big dog. During his remarkable career as a rescue dog, Barry, a Saint Bernard, saved the lives of forty people lost on the snowy peaks of the Swiss Alps in the treacherous Great St Bernard Pass, which connects the countries of Switzerland and Italy. Although difficult to travel at eight thousand feet, this snow-packed pass became an important military and trade route. Barry was bred and trained by the monks of the Great St Bernard Hospice, which offered food, shelter, and medical care to weary pilgrims traveling from Switzerland to Rome in Italy. The dogs didn't carry brandy kegs around their necks as depicted in many illustrations. Instead, Barry carried bread and water in saddlebags that hung across his back. With his keen sense of smell and a good sense of direction, Barry could locate a lost traveler even in a blinding blizzard. He would then dig the man out of the snow and ice, lying down beside him to restore body heat.

Often these large dogs were sent out by twos and threes. One or two dogs would lie down next to a traveler to keep him warm while another returned to the hospice to get help. The work was dangerous. Many of the dogs died, killed by avalanches while attempting a rescue. The Saint Bernards made excellent guide dogs too, pushing through the deep snow with their broad chests. They were so successful in their work that when the emperor Napoleon crossed the Alps in the year 1800 with thousands of soldiers, he didn't lose a single man.

Today, lost travelers are rescued by helicopter, but Switzerland's Barry Foundation continues to breed Saint Bernards to be used as therapy dogs. Each year one puppy is named Barry in honor of the courageous canine who became a legend in his own time.

SOMETHING TO THINK ABOUT

Did you know the famous Saint Bernard puppies learned rescue techniques by following the example of older dogs? At first, they just tagged along and watched what the big dogs did. Soon they were rescuing stranded travelers on their own and showing younger dogs how to do the same.

You can learn things by watching older Christians serving the Lord. Offer to help, working alongside them. Ask questions if you have them. The writer of Ecclesiastes advises his readers, "Remember your Creator in the days of your youth, before the days of trouble come" (12:1).

*Lord, thank You for those believers who serve You
so faithfully and serve as role models for young
people like me. In Jesus's name, amen.*

A CIRCLE OF SEALS

Friendly Rescuers

1999

When Charlene Camburn, her friend Chris, and her seven-year-old son, Brogan, visited the Donna Nook nature preserve along the coast of England on the North Sea, they became trapped on a sandbar. Enchanted by the spectacle of sea birds and the colony of gray seals, they'd failed to notice the fog and tide rushing in. They could no longer see the grassy marshlands. They now appeared to be surrounded by water. Brogan and Chris couldn't swim, so Charlene decided to seek help. She plunged into the icy sea and swam for shore. But as late afternoon turned to evening, she became disoriented in the gloom. The current grew stronger. Her teeth chattered. More than an hour had passed. Exhausted and cold, Charlene feared she might never see Brogan and Chris again. She prayed for their safety. She prayed for strength to make it to shore.

Suddenly, six gray seals surrounded her, squeaking and barking. They peered into her face. Charlene knew seals could be aggressively territorial, especially when they had young seal pups to protect. But these creatures behaved in a friendly manner. She felt mildly relieved. She also despaired, convinced that by now Brogan and Chris had surely drowned. Too cold and tired to swim any longer, Charlene sank beneath the waves. That's when the seal squad came to her rescue. They dove underneath her feet, pushing her back to the surface. When Charlene passed out, the seals kept her afloat.

In the meantime, Brogan and Chris had discovered a finger of dry land. They quickly followed it to shore, where they contacted the Coast Guard. Soon the rescue boat located Charlene. As lights from the rescue boat pierced the darkness, the men onboard found her barely conscious and surrounded by a circle of protective seals. Charlene was rushed to a hospital, where she was treated for hypothermia and reunited with Brogan and Chris. She'd been in the icy sea for two hours. Her rescuers found it remarkable that she'd survived the ordeal. Had it not been for the seals encircling her, she would have drifted farther out to sea and surely drowned. Everyone was even more astonished when Charlene explained how the seals had kept her afloat. She freely admitted they'd saved her life.

SOMETHING TO THINK ABOUT

No one could explain why these creatures came to Charlene's rescue. Some surmised the seals were simply curious. Others suggest they wanted to play with Charlene. Still, there are those who recognize this as a near miracle. The fact remains, the seals saved Charlene's life.

Perhaps you need help or comfort now too. God knows. He hears your prayers and will send helpers to assist you, to pray with you, and pray for you.

Lord, I believe in You. I am trusting You to help me. When I'm scared or sad or worried, hold me close. In Jesus's name, amen.

TOGO

Nome Hero

1925

Heavy snow. Gale-force winds. Dangerous ice floes. Leonhard Seppala and his dog Togo battled them all during their extraordinary Alaskan journey to bring lifesaving serum to Nome.

In January 1925, several children living in Nome died from deadly diphtheria. Everyone feared more people would die if they couldn't obtain the antitoxin. The town's desperate doctor sent a telegram requesting help. An Anchorage hospital agreed to provide thousands of units of vaccine, but ships were icebound. Heavy snow made the roads impassable. Icy winds prevented air travel. Their only hope was the old-fashioned method—men with dogsleds.

Seppala was the territory's most famous musher, or dogsled racer. He was known as "King of the Trail." He and his lead dog, Togo—a Siberian husky—had won nearly every race they had entered. But at the age of forty-seven, Seppala was considered past his prime. Togo was aging, too, and small for the breed. But Seppala's young daughter lived in Nome. She might die if something wasn't done quickly.

So Seppala helped organize several dogsled relay teams and

mapped out a route across frozen lakes and icy tundra and through dense forests. Soon the epic Nome serum run was underway. Twenty drivers and 150 dogs participated. It usually took men and dogs twenty-five days to travel the 675-mile route to deliver mail between Fairbanks and Nome. The hard-pressed relay teams would complete the task in a miraculous six days despite blizzard conditions. Some of the mushers lost fingers and toes to frostbite. Many dogs died along the way.

Seppala took the longest, most treacherous leg of the route—ninety-one miles—with Togo leading the dog team. Both Seppala and Togo were tough, smart, and determined. When Seppala passed the precious serum canister to Gunnar Kaasen and his dog Balto, their team finished the race and were hailed as heroes in Nome. The heroism of the men and dogs captivated the entire country. Balto received most of the credit and fame as well as special recognition from President Calvin Coolidge. At first Seppala didn't mind that Kaasen and Balto were offered a Hollywood movie deal and opportunities to travel across the United States talking about the race. But when a bronze statue of Balto was unveiled in New York's Central Park, Seppala resented it. He believed Togo deserved the recognition.

In 1973, a sporting race known as the Iditarod began. The dogs and mushers follow the same approximate route as the "Great Race of Mercy." Today, Togo's mounted body is on display at the Iditarod headquarters, and veterinarians present the Leonhard Seppala Humanitarian Award to the musher who takes the best care of his dogs. And yes, now there is a statue of Togo in New York City.

TOGO

Nome Hero

1925

Heavy snow. Gale-force winds. Dangerous ice floes. Leonhard Seppala and his dog Togo battled them all during their extraordinary Alaskan journey to bring lifesaving serum to Nome.

In January 1925, several children living in Nome died from deadly diphtheria. Everyone feared more people would die if they couldn't obtain the antitoxin. The town's desperate doctor sent a telegram requesting help. An Anchorage hospital agreed to provide thousands of units of vaccine, but ships were icebound. Heavy snow made the roads impassable. Icy winds prevented air travel. Their only hope was the old-fashioned method—men with dogsleds.

Seppala was the territory's most famous musher, or dogsled racer. He was known as "King of the Trail." He and his lead dog, Togo—a Siberian husky—had won nearly every race they had entered. But at the age of forty-seven, Seppala was considered past his prime. Togo was aging, too, and small for the breed. But Seppala's young daughter lived in Nome. She might die if something wasn't done quickly.

So Seppala helped organize several dogsled relay teams and

mapped out a route across frozen lakes and icy tundra and through dense forests. Soon the epic Nome serum run was underway. Twenty drivers and 150 dogs participated. It usually took men and dogs twenty-five days to travel the 675-mile route to deliver mail between Fairbanks and Nome. The hard-pressed relay teams would complete the task in a miraculous six days despite blizzard conditions. Some of the mushers lost fingers and toes to frostbite. Many dogs died along the way.

Seppala took the longest, most treacherous leg of the route—ninety-one miles—with Togo leading the dog team. Both Seppala and Togo were tough, smart, and determined. When Seppala passed the precious serum canister to Gunnar Kaasen and his dog Balto, their team finished the race and were hailed as heroes in Nome. The heroism of the men and dogs captivated the entire country. Balto received most of the credit and fame as well as special recognition from President Calvin Coolidge. At first Seppala didn't mind that Kaasen and Balto were offered a Hollywood movie deal and opportunities to travel across the United States talking about the race. But when a bronze statue of Balto was unveiled in New York's Central Park, Seppala resented it. He believed Togo deserved the recognition.

In 1973, a sporting race known as the Iditarod began. The dogs and mushers follow the same approximate route as the "Great Race of Mercy." Today, Togo's mounted body is on display at the Iditarod headquarters, and veterinarians present the Leonhard Seppala Humanitarian Award to the musher who takes the best care of his dogs. And yes, now there is a statue of Togo in New York City.

SOMETHING TO THINK ABOUT

Leonhard Seppala and Togo—as well as the other men and dogs in the famous serum race—had the awesome responsibility of saving lives. All were uniquely equipped to fulfill that task. Whatever God's purpose for your life is, be assured He will equip you to do it.

Dear Lord, give me the courage to do the things
You would have me do. In Jesus's name, amen.

SIMON

Courageous Rat Catcher

1949

I n 1949, a seventeen-year-old British sailor named George Hickinbottom scooped up a hungry stray in Hong Kong and smuggled the scrawny black-and-white kitten onto the *HMS Amethyst*. The rat problem on board the ship was miserable. Vermin spread disease and threatened the men's food supply. Hickinbottom hoped Simon could help.

The cat proved to be a champion rat catcher. He often placed his "trophy" on a man's bunk or by the captain's shoe. Impressed with Simon's achievements, the crew kept track of Simon's kills on a chart. The cat's presence raised morale. Everyone loved Simon—even the captain, who allowed the friendly feline to nap in his white, gold-braided hat when he wasn't wearing it. He tolerated the cat's meandering across the naval charts when the officers tried to plot a course.

One day while the *Amethyst* patrolled the Yangtze River in China, Mao Tse-tung's Communist troops fired on the ship. The captain and several crew members were killed, and many others were wounded. Even Simon suffered severe injuries. The crew were held hostage on their battered ship for months, during which time the medical officer worked to save Simon's life.

The cat's recovery cheered the battle-weary hostages. Following the shelling of the ship, the rat problem became even worse. Vermin scuttled through the air vents and down the corridors. One large, menacing rat attacked several sleeping men in their bunks. Simon returned to rat patrol full-time. When he killed the huge rat the sailors had dubbed Mini-Mao, the grateful crew officially promoted Simon to Able Seaman.

With food and water supplies dwindling, the sailors suffered from hunger and dehydration. The new captain hatched a daring plan. One moonless night under the cover of darkness, the crew of the *Amethyst* escaped. When their battered ship returned to Hong Kong harbor, the men were hailed as heroes. Newspapers and newsreels around the world reported their daring exploits. Simon became a celebrity too and posed for photos with his shipmates. A "cat officer" took charge of Simon's fan mail, telegrams, gifts of tinned food, and checks to purchase cream for the hero feline. The crew rejoiced when they learned Simon was to receive a Dickin Medal from the People's Dispensary for Sick Animals. Sadly, Simon died before the ceremony, his heart weakened by his war injuries. The grieving crew buried Simon with military honors.

SOMETHING TO THINK ABOUT

Have you ever felt like a hostage of fear and trouble? We may never face the same difficulties that Simon and the crew of the *Amethyst* did, but whatever our circumstances, we can pray for God's protection. He always hears our prayers.

Dear Jesus, please protect me in times of trouble, when I am afraid and don't know what to do. Support me with Your strength and grace and keep me mindful of Your presence. In Your name, I ask it, amen.

BANDOOLA

Elephant Hero

1944

Elephants usually don't climb mountains—especially powerful tuskers trained to haul lumber through the Burmese jungles. But during World War II, a remarkable elephant named Bandoola did just that, leading a band of desperate refugees to safety in India.

Bandoola was as smart as he was strong. Po Toke, his *oozie*, or elephant handler, enjoyed having Bandoola show off his intelligence. Po Toke would line up a hammer, a saw, chains, and an axe. Then he'd say to Bandoola, "Please hand me the saw." The elephant always handed the man exactly the tool he asked for. Trained for years with kindness and gentleness, Bandoola developed a bond of affection and trust with Po Toke, which became especially important during the war years.

In March 1944, Lieutenant Colonel John H. Williams and his fellow British officers in the elephant corps received urgent orders to evacuate their working elephants out of Burma (now Myanmar) before the invading Japanese troops could capture them. As they prepared for their flight to freedom, Bandoola was dubbed Number 1 War Elephant and chosen to lead the desperate procession, which included 198 men, women, and children, 45 elephants, and 8 elephant calves.

With gritty determination, Bandoola and Po Toke led the way. The exhausting, hundred-mile journey took nineteen days. At one point, they encountered a sheer 270-foot cliff. Under Po Toke's calm guidance, Bandoola climbed to the top along a narrow ledge. Po Toke rode on the elephant's massive head, carefully directing the tusker's slow, hesitant steps. The other elephants bravely followed their leader. So great was the strain during this dangerous climb that the animals' leg muscles shook for nearly an hour afterward.

When several of the small children became ill with fever on the journey, they were placed carefully in large baskets draped across Bandoola's broad back. The powerful elephant seemed to realize he carried a fragile cargo and behaved accordingly. Upon their safe arrival at a tea plantation near Silchar, India, Lieutenant Colonel Williams offered a prayer of thanksgiving. He later wrote two books, *Elephant Bill* and *Bandoola*, relating his adventures with Bandoola and the other praiseworthy pachyderms that had marched with him on the retreat.

SOMETHING TO THINK ABOUT

Bandoola and Po Toke were champions of cooperation. It took trust and endurance for both elephants and people to safely travel this dangerous escape route.

Have you ever prayed for strength when you faced a difficult task? King David did. He wrote, "I lift up my eyes to the mountains—where does my help come from? My help comes from the LORD, the Maker of heaven and earth" (Psalm 121:1-2).

Father in heaven, help me to cooperate with the people in my family and at school. I want to be a champion of faith for You. In Jesus's name, amen.

BERT

Camel Champ

2018

amels have a bad reputation. They are cranky and stinky. They spit. But Bert is different—really different. The one-hump dromedary is protective and gentle. He loves children, elderly people, and Skittles candy. He was sworn in as a deputy sergeant with the Los Angeles Sheriff's Department. He even has a badge and a uniform with a hole at the top so his hump can stick out. His name stands for Be Enthusiastic, Responsible, and True. Bert and his handler, Reserve Deputy Nance Fite, have visited dozens of elementary schools to teach students about good citizenship and to caution them to stay away from drugs. Bert was named the highest-ranking law-enforcement camel in *Guinness World Records 2018*.

Bert marches in parades and surprises people at parties. He's also a bit of a trickster and has been known to stick his big nose into bags to snatch kids' Halloween candy or swipe the hat off a man's head with his teeth. But Nance insists it's Bert's amazing instincts and his compassion that make this camel one of a kind. These virtues in a two-thousand-pound camel are hard to explain. He lets blind children dig their fingers into his furry neck. He serves as a congenial icebreaker in rough neighborhoods by making a loud, guttural sound as he kisses a child on the head.

Occasionally, Bert makes hospital visits to bring a little happiness to the sad and sick patients there. Once he laid his huge furry head in the lap of a little boy in a wheelchair. Hardly able to move, the child had been very ill and unresponsive for months. Bert remained motionless and patient. The boy struggled to raise his hand to pet Bert. Then the boy giggled. Nance and the nurses and other adults watched this encounter with joyful tears. Nance declared, "I think that moment is why Bert was put on this earth."

SOMETHING TO THINK ABOUT

When it comes to displaying compassion, Bert is a champ. Do you know what it means to be compassionate? It means showing pity and concern for the suffering and misfortunes of others. In 1 Peter 3:8, the apostle urges believers to be compassionate. Bert is a gentle, caring camel. God created him that way. What about you? Do you show compassion for others?

Lord, help me to be a more compassionate person. And thank You for the people in my life who have been patient and kind with me. In Jesus's name, amen.

ANTIS

Flying Ace

1949

When Czech air gunner Robert Bozděch rescued a starving Alsatian puppy from a bombed-out farmhouse in Germany during World War II, he had no idea Antis would fly into aviation history. Back at the Allied airbase, Antis earned the nickname "Radar Dog" because of his ability to suspect aerial attacks even before radar detected the incoming enemy aircraft. Whining loudly, Antis would turn his face up to the sky, fixing his gaze on the horizon. Allied airmen learned to heed his warning. Sometimes, even after the "all clear" siren sounded, Antis whined and barked a warning. He could tell that more enemy aircraft were still on their way. Robert and the other men learned to trust the dog's instincts. Antis is credited with saving countless lives, including Robert's. The grateful men lavished their canine hero with food and affection.

Antis accompanied Robert on thirty air missions over enemy territory. He was even fitted with a special oxygen mask. He never whined or panicked when in flight, even when he was seriously wounded by shrapnel and lay bleeding at Robert's feet. Once, their plane was shot down by enemy aircraft and plunged into the sea. Robert swam with Antis on his back until they were rescued by a British warship.

After the war, Robert returned to his homeland, hailed as a hero. But peace didn't last long. Communists took over Czechoslovakia. Peace-loving Czech citizens like Robert who'd fought with the Allies during the war were arrested as criminals, so Robert and Antis escaped back to England. The journey through the Iron Curtain was a dangerous one. Antis saved Robert's life again when he attacked and pinned down an armed border guard. Safely back in London, Antis received Great Britain's prestigious Dickin medal in 1949. He was the first "foreign" dog to receive the honor.

SOMETHING TO THINK ABOUT

Antis and Robert remained faithful friends for thirteen years. They lived during difficult times. Many people were forced to live behind the Iron Curtain—a name for Communist-controlled European countries where people were not allowed to come and go freely. Communists do not believe in God or His Son, Jesus, and often persecute or punish people who do. Today there are still many people living under Communist governments.

Often, it's hard to focus on the Lord when we are stressed, afraid, and distracted. Remember to give Jesus all your troubles and concerns because He cares for you.

Dear Lord, please protect our Christian brothers and sisters living in Communist-controlled countries. Give them hope and surround them with Your peace. In Jesus's name, amen.

HUBERTA

Adventurous Hippo

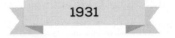

1931

Why did the hippopotamus cross the road?

To get to the other side?

No one knows why Huberta the hippopotamus made her epic trek along the coastline of South Africa. She left her watering hole in the Saint Lucia Estuary to waddle south for nearly three years. Normally, hippos stay within six or seven miles of their home base. Huberta didn't fit the mold. She bravely traveled more than a thousand miles throughout the country, crossing 122 rivers during her amazing journey. She walked mostly at night to avoid crowds of people. Her strange journey made newspaper headlines around the world.

No one knew where the roaming hippo might appear next. Once she was discovered in a field feasting on sugar cane. Then she took a nap on the railroad tracks. An amused train crew woke her with a nudge from the cowcatcher on the front of the locomotive. Another time she moseyed onto a country-club veranda, where a party was in progress. The astonished guests assumed Huberta's appearance was a party prank. They watched with amusement as Huberta waddled across the golf course, disappearing into the night.

By 1931, bold Huberta was declared a national heroine. The Natal Provincial Council even issued a decree protecting her under law. After her death, the hippo's bulky body was preserved. Thousands of fans attended a ceremony to see Huberta's remains put on display in a museum.

SOMETHING TO THINK ABOUT

Huberta's adventurous spirit touched people in a way that's hard to explain. Perhaps they realized how much courage it took for the hippopotamus to leave her natural habitat, to do something that hippos normally don't do. Perhaps that's why most of us admire missionaries and explorers. They take risks the rest of us don't.

Have you ever longed for a daring adventure? Perhaps something simple, like zip-lining through a rainforest? Or perhaps something more daring, like going to the Philippines on a mission trip? Most adventures take a certain amount of courage. What adventure does God have in store for you?

Lord, give me the courage to be adventurous
for You. In Jesus's name, amen.

JAKE

Ground Zero Hero

2001

sn't it amazing how often animal heroes begin their lives in sadness and difficulty? Jake, a black Labrador retriever, had been abandoned as a puppy with a broken leg and a dislocated hip. But Mary Flood, a member of Utah Task Force I—a federal search-and-rescue team—found him and adopted him. After seeking medical attention for Jake, Mary nursed him back to full health with tender loving care. When he recovered, she trained Jake to become one of the nation's elite search-and-rescue dogs. Mary knew Jake would perform well: He had courage and a strong survival instinct. She'd watched how determined he was to overcome his injuries.

Jake accompanied the team to disaster sites across the country, helping to rescue survivors of floods, earthquakes, hurricanes, and avalanches. This elite team needs to be ready at a moment's notice to travel to the site of a catastrophe. Jake's toughest assignment came in 2001 when he searched for survivors of the 9/11 disaster at the World Trade Center in New York City. One of three hundred rescue dogs, Jake worked in brutal conditions during each twelve-hour shift, trying to locate survivors beneath the razor-sharp rubble at Ground Zero. Veterinarians cleaned his eyes, nose, and paws during rest periods. Jake and the other dogs were hailed as heroes. When Jake, wearing his search-and-rescue vest, entered a fancy Manhattan restaurant with Mary for a meal, Jake received a free steak dinner under the table.

In 2005, Mary and Jake drove from Utah to Mississippi to help locate survivors of Hurricane Katrina. Jake never hesitated to perform his duties no matter how difficult or dangerous the circumstances. Jake even proved useful in training the next generation of rescue pups. He showed them how to detect scents in all sorts of weather conditions. Jake even showed the younger dogs how to sniff out something high up in a tree!

When Jake died in 2007 at the age of twelve, the death of this Ground Zero hero was reported in newspapers around the world. Mary scattered Jake's ashes in the Utah hills, where he used to romp as a puppy.

SOMETHING TO THINK ABOUT

After Jake had been rescued as a crippled stray, he grew up to become an important member of a special rescue team. Have you ever been on a winning team—perhaps in sports or a dance troupe? Maybe a chess team that has taken first or second place in a regional competition? Being a part of a winning team is fun, isn't it! Just remember, even when you don't win, you're still special to God. He made you unique. There's no one else in the world like you.

Thank You, Lord, for true-life stories like Jake's. It's wonderful to see how You can bring triumph out of tragedy. You're amazing! In Jesus's name, amen.

SNOWMAN

Who Never Gave Up

1958

ometimes no one realizes how courageous an animal is. That's what happened with one dirty, gray plow horse. When no one bought him at auction, he was loaded onto a truck headed for the slaughterhouse. Harry deLeyer, a New York riding instructor, attended the auction hoping to buy a gentle horse for his beginning students. He came too late to buy one of the good horses. The only one left was Snowman. The plow horse had kind eyes. Harry thought he might be gentle enough for young riders, so he bought the horse for eighty dollars.

Snowman proved to be a good mount for children. He liked being around them and never reacted when they pulled his tail or tugged on his mane. Harry sold him anyway to a neighbor when the man offered to pay twice what Harry had paid for the horse. But Snowman didn't want to leave Harry. The next day, the horse jumped the fence to return home. The fence was five feet high. Snowman did this several times. Once he even returned dragging a large log and a thirty-foot halter. Harry chuckled and took the homesick horse back. Curious, he wondered if Snowman could be trained as a jumper. They practiced together for two years. Snowman loved jumping! He was brave too, willing to jump higher and higher obstacles. He never got tired of practicing.

People laughed when Harry entered the former plow horse in a jumping contest. They stopped laughing when the pair won the 1958 Open Jumper Championship at Madison Square Garden's Diamond Jubilee. Everyone *oohed* and *aahed* when Snowman won again in 1959—the first horse to win the championship two years in a row. He was now a superstar! Snowman's hard work and success inspired many people over the years. When Snowman passed away in 1974, Harry was there, sitting right by his side.

SOMETHING TO THINK ABOUT

Have you ever noticed that horses come in all sorts of colors? Snowman appears white in his photographs, but he was really considered gray. There are shades of dappled gray, pearl and mushroom, black and smoky black, brown, chestnut, buckskin, pinto, and even red roan. There are too many horse colors and horse breeds to list here. God the Creator has quite an imagination. He could have made horses all the same size and color, but He didn't. Isn't He amazing?

Thank You, Lord, for all the beautiful horses and for all the other wonderful creatures You have made. We can know You exist just by looking at the amazing world around us. We praise You in Jesus's name, amen.

KHAN

The Wonder Dog

2007

Khan suffered from starvation. He had broken ribs and other signs of abuse when Catherine Svilicic in Australia decided to adopt the Doberman pinscher that shelter workers had considered euthanizing. Something about the dog tugged at her heart. Catherine hoped he'd make a good pet.

Khan had been with Catherine's family for only four days when he did something extraordinary. While exploring the backyard with Catherine's toddler Charlotte, Khan began to act aggressively. He pushed the baby with his snout. When Charlotte ignored him, Khan snatched her by the diaper and flung her over his shoulder as though she were nothing more than a doll. She landed with a thud a short distance away—unharmed—but Khan yowled in pain. A king brown snake—one of the most poisonous snakes in the world—had lunged forward, sinking its fangs into Khan's paw. The dog collapsed as he tried to make it back to the house.

Realizing that Khan had saved her child, Catherine rushed the canine hero to a veterinarian, where he received a shot of antivenin. To the family's relief, Khan recovered in a few days. An expert explained that because the snake had bitten Khan's thin paw, it had not been able to release a full amount of poison. Had the snake bitten Charlotte's leg, however, the story could have had a very tragic ending.

Catherine dubbed her brave pet the Wonder Dog. People hearing of his bravery wondered, had Khan instinctively protected Charlotte because she was a child? Or was Khan grateful for being rescued from the shelter and decided to return the favor by rescuing Charlotte? No one knows for sure.

SOMETHING TO THINK ABOUT

The Svilicic family vowed to cherish Khan for the rest of his life. That's how they will show their gratitude to Khan for rescuing Charlotte. But did Khan save Charlotte's life in gratitude for being rescued from the shelter? Was Khan happy to be chosen from all the other dogs there?

Most of us enjoy the thrill of being chosen—chosen to play on a team, chosen for an important role in a theater production, chosen to sing a solo in the choir. But just remember this: God has chosen you too! You are a one-of-a-kind creation. There's no one else in the world just like you.

Dear Lord, thank You for choosing to love me before I ever knew about You. And thank You for sending Your Son, Jesus, to die for me. In His name I pray, amen.

SERGEANT BILLY

Goat Hero

1915

Would you willingly give up your pet to be a mascot for a military platoon? That's what a Canadian girl named Daisy did during World War I when the soldiers of the 5th Canadian Infantry Battalion Mounted Rifles asked if they could take her pet goat with them "for luck" when they were shipped overseas. Feeling patriotic and wanting to help the soldiers, Daisy agreed to let Billy go to war. But the men's commanding officer didn't like the idea at all. He refused to take Billy along. The soldiers jokingly agreed that they could always get a new colonel, but finding another lucky goat wouldn't be so easy. Determined to take their mascot with them, the soldiers hid Billy inside a wagon underneath a tarp and then smuggled the goat aboard ship before sailing across the Atlantic Ocean to France.

Unfortunately, Billy was not an ideal mascot. He proved to be quite a nuisance at first. He ate everything in sight, even important military documents. When a high-ranking officer tried to rescue the important papers, Billy headbutted him out of the tent. Billy also caught trench foot—a disease caused by moisture that made his feet swell painfully. He sustained injuries from flying shrapnel and had to receive medical treatment. He even suffered shell shock following one particularly brutal battle.

But one day, Billy finally proved his worth. He cornered an enemy soldier hiding in a bomb crater until the men of the Fighting 5th captured the terrified spy. On another day, Billy headbutted three soldiers into a trench just seconds before a shell exploded where they'd been standing. All agreed the quick-reacting goat had saved their lives. Billy was promoted to sergeant on the spot. Later he was presented with a special blanket resembling the regimental uniform—complete with medals and badges of honor. After the war, the goat returned to Canada with the regiment. He led the soldiers in a victory parade. Billy lived out his life with Daisy, who was proud of her courageous pet and pleased to have him home again.

SOMETHING TO THINK ABOUT

War heroes shine like a light of hope in dark times. Sergeant Billy boosted his buddies' morale too. Hebrews 3:13 advises us to "encourage one another daily" (NASB). You can be a brother or sister of encouragement too even if you're not fighting in a war. Choosing to do the right thing—even when it's hard—is one way you can be an inspiration to those around you.

Lord, help me to be an encouragement to others. Show me what to say or do. I want to be like You. In Jesus's name, amen.

GI JOE

Fearless Messenger

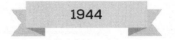

1944

G I Joe, a pigeon that served in the Unites States Army Pigeon Service, was the first American animal to receive Britain's prestigious Dickin Medal.

British soldiers of the 56th Brigade in Italy were trying to call off a bombing raid planned by their American allies. The town had surrendered. The Nazis had fled. There was no need for the bombers to come. If the Americans carried out their mission as planned, many British soldiers and Italian civilians would be killed or injured. They had to stop those planes!

But with telegraph lines down and their radio broken, the British soldiers had just one last hope. A message explaining their situation was placed into a small tube attached to Joe's leg. The bird made the twenty-mile flight in twenty minutes. He arrived in the nick of time too: The American fighter pilots were already climbing into their planes. Another message was quickly tucked inside Joe's tiny tube, and the bird was sent back to the 56th Brigade with the good news that the bombing raid had been called off. The soldiers and relieved townspeople cheered! Joe's swift flight had saved the lives of the British troops and countless Italian civilians.

When the war ended in 1945, the grateful British government honored GI Joe with a medal. The hero bird traveled to England, where he was met at the airport by both American and British officials and treated as an honored guest. The special ceremony was attended by reporters, photographers, radio commentators, several high-ranking generals, and the Lord Mayor of London. No other war bird has ever received such a remarkable day of honor. Following the festivities, Joe was flown back to the United States. He lived out the remainder of his long life in the Detroit Zoo, where hundreds of visitors came to admire the hero in residence.

SOMETHING TO THINK ABOUT

GI Joe was a reliable helper for the military personnel who depended on him. Sometimes it's hard to be reliable, especially when you're scared or worried or busy with too many things. It's also easy to get distracted and forget that you promised to finish your homework or clean your room like you said you would. You can trust Jesus to help you stay focused. Just ask Him.

Dear Lord, support me with Your strength and grace, and help me to be reliable—especially when I'm tired or worried or super busy with lots to do. In Jesus's name, amen.

SHERLOCK

Dog Detective

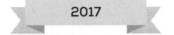

2017

A sweet-faced cocker spaniel named Sherlock is an important member of the London Fire Brigade's investigation and rescue team in England. He even has an official job title: specialist fire investigation dog. This doggie detective investigates 180 to 230 fire incidents each year. Sherlock has been trained to sniff out ten different ignitable liquids, including gasoline, acetone, paraffin, and lighter fluid. These items are often used by arsonists—criminals who deliberately set fires in buildings. Sherlock can sniff out substances even after they have evaporated or been burned up because of extreme heat—up to a year after the blaze! It takes a special machine eight to ten hours to detect what Sherlock can do in just two minutes!

Even after a fire is put out, Sherlock's work is still dangerous. He must wear special red boots to protect his feet. After a burned building has cooled, Sherlock's handler goes in first to assess any possible hazards. Damaged electrical wiring, broken glass, and falling debris are just a few of the dangers. Once Sherlock was sent to the site of a rugby clubhouse that had burned to the ground. The ruined site was huge, but Sherlock tackled the job quickly. He located the accelerant, which proved to be the sort of flammable fluid used to ignite a barbecue grill. Thanks to Sherlock's sharp nose, the authorities were able to link the blaze to other arson cases and arrest a suspect. Sherlock was the hero of the day!

Boasting a 100 percent success rate, Sherlock's nose has proven to be more accurate than modern technology, saving time and money for the police department and the fire brigade. Sherlock's high level of accuracy helps lead to the conviction of criminals who start the fires. And what sort of reward does Sherlock enjoy after a successful case is wrapped up? A tennis ball. Yep, a tennis ball—his favorite treat. Every time he identifies an ignitable liquid, Sherlock receives a tennis ball to play with.

Because of his courage and outstanding performance, Sherlock earned the Animal Hero Award from the Royal Society for the Prevention of Cruelty to Animals in 2017.

SOMETHING TO THINK ABOUT

Isn't it amazing to think that the skills of a dog like Sherlock can be more efficient than our modern technology? Dogs also helped fire departments long ago, when fast horses pulled the engines and firemen through the crowded streets. Many departments had dalmatians that ran in front of the horses, barking and howling to clear a path. Often the dogs had to protect the horses from being bit by stray dogs that chased after them down the street.

And guess what? God can use you too in many situations where modern technology just won't suffice. After all, sometimes a friend needs a hug—and a text message just won't do!

Dear Lord, thank You for this day and for the gift of life. I am excited and curious to find out how You might use my special gifts and talents for Your glory. In Jesus's name, amen.

ld and weak to follow. Sensing their distress, Shana wriggled
ack through the tunnel toward them. Using her teeth, Shana
ipped Eve's jacket, yanking the frail eighty-six-pound woman
nto her broad back. Norman grabbed his wife's legs and held on
ght. Again, Shana inched her way through the tunnel toward
e house, slowly towing the couple to safety—a feat that took
ore than two hours.

Home at last, Eve and Norman staggered to their feet and
ottered wearily into the house. Because of the storm, they had
o heat, no electricity, and no hot water. Concerned neighbors,
nable to reach the couple by phone, called the fire department.
he next morning firemen discovered the exhausted Fertigs alive
nd well, huddled together on the floor, with Shana lying beside
hem to keep them warm.

Amazed by the couple's rescue story, the firemen went into
he backyard to examine Shana's remarkable tunnel. They'd never
een anything like it. Although the elderly couple quickly recov-
red from their ordeal, Shana sustained serious injuries to her legs
nd paws while digging the tunnel. These injuries took months to
roperly heal, but the Fertigs took good care of their beloved hero.
Shana received several awards for her brave rescue effort, includ-
ng a plaque from the local firefighters who'd been so impressed
by Shana's heroic behavior.

DYLAN

Courageous Cockatiel

2014

Have you ever seen a cockatiel? These cute birds are smart
and friendly. They have jaunty crested topknots on their
heads and rosy cheeks. Andy Hardiek of Indiana owned
a pet cockatiel named Dylan, who proved to be a fine feathered
hero. One night after a long, exhausting shift at work, Andy
returned home and went straight to bed. He fell into a deep sleep,
unaware that the heat tape wrapped around the pipes underneath
his mobile home had caught on fire, filling the trailer with harm-
ful fumes and deadly flames.

At first, the smoke detectors didn't alert him to the danger.
That's when Dylan came to the rescue. The bird jumped up and
down, squawking loudly. He rattled his cage. He squawked even
louder. Finally, Andy woke up. He smelled the smoke and saw
the fire blazing in the next room. Andy quickly reached for the
fire extinguisher but soon realized it was already too dangerous
to remain inside. If he was going to get out alive, he needed to
do so at once. Grabbing Dylan's cage, Andy dashed outside to
safety. He freely admitted later that had it not been for his noisy
bird buddy, he would have died in the blaze. The fire chief later
agreed, praising Dylan for being a successful fire alarm.

SOMETHING TO THINK ABOUT

Sadly, Andy's home and all his possessions were destroyed. But he was grateful to be alive. Life is more important than things.

How would you respond to losing everything you own? Sometimes people put too much value on their possessions. They want to buy more and more stuff. There are even those who believe that security is found in the amount of money they possess. Anchor your hope in Jesus Christ and the treasures He has for you in heaven, not on things of this world.

Dear Lord, help me to surrender all I have to You and not be anxious about owning things. In Jesus's name, amen.

SHANA

Tireless Tunneler

2006

One crisp October evening, Eve and Norma eighty-one years old, went out to feed the inj their backyard wildlife sanctuary in New Y a burly 160-pound timber wolf–German shepherd fully dogged their steps. The elderly couple had re as a pup from a cruel breeder who'd planned to vicious dog fights.

As the Fertigs went about feeding the injured and kestrels in their care, a fierce storm blew in, bri snow and bitterly cold wind. The couple suddenly selves trapped by fallen trees in a narrow alley betwee buildings. They couldn't crawl over the trees or mak around them. Wearing only light jackets, they huddl for warmth. As the snow continued to pile up and fell, the Fertigs feared they might die.

That's when Shana came to their rescue. Using her claws, she dug a twenty-foot tunnel underneath the through the heavy snow all the way to the Fertigs' b Hours later, Shana barked from the far end of the tunne telling them to crawl out after her. But Eve and Norma

SOMETHING TO THINK ABOUT

Occasionally, we may experience hard times that make us feel scared. We worry that God is not with us. But He is! You can trust Him always. As Eve Fertig declared in an interview following her ordeal, "God is watching; He's watching all the time."

Father in heaven, help us to remember You are with us always—even in the scary times. In Jesus's name, amen.

WOJTEK

Soldier Bear

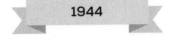

D o you own a teddy bear? Can you imagine what it might be like to cuddle your very own real-life bear?

During World War II, Polish Lance Corporal Peter Prendys rescued a tiny bear cub while stationed in Iran. Peter named the cub Wojtek (pronounced Voy-check), which means "smiling warrior" in Polish. The cub became the mascot of the Polish 22nd Transport Company. Peter fed him condensed milk and provided him with an old wash tub to sleep in. Wojtek became so attached to Peter that the cub cried like a baby whenever Peter was out of sight.

Wojtek liked to ride with Peter in the front seat of the transport truck. He raided food pantries looking for jam, fruit, and honey. He once provoked the wrath of the women in the military Signal Corps when he pulled all their clean underwear off a clothesline and wrapped the garments around his head and neck— shredding most of them in the process. Another day he waddled to the shower hut and discovered the door was open. Inside, the bear frightened an Arab spy who had crept unseen into the camp. Wojtek kept the man cowering in the corner until help arrived.

During the brutal battle of Monte Cassino in Italy, Wojtek

witnessed serious action for the first time and earned his legendary status. He stayed close to Peter and soon got used to the noise
of planes roaring overhead and bombs exploding. The Polish
transport troops lugged seventeen thousand tons of ammo and
one thousand pounds of food to the front lines during the battle.

Wojtek watched Peter and the other men. One morning he
waddled on his hind legs to a truck, holding out his front paws.
When a man handed him a twenty-five-pound artillery shell,
Wojtek carried it to the fighting soldiers. He continued to work
unsupervised throughout the battle. American and British soldiers gasped with astonishment at the sight of the huge brown
bear walking upright, effortlessly carrying boxes of ammunition
and huge cannon shells.

After this battle, a special badge depicting Wojtek carrying
an artillery shell became one of the most sought-after military
insignias of the war. When the war was over, Wojtek accompanied the Polish troops to Glasgow in Scotland, where he marched
like a soldier during the victory parade. Today Wojtek remains
an inspirational symbol of Polish unity.

SOMETHING TO THINK ABOUT

Surprisingly, Wojtek never turned savage when he became a full-grown bear. Instead, he modeled his behavior after the men he lived with.

Jesus's twelve handpicked disciples followed Him for three years watching Him pray, listening to Him preach, and learning how to heal the sick and interact with all sorts of people. They, in turn, taught others how to live as Christ would have us live.

Who models Christian behavior for you? You can learn a lot by serving alongside other believers who are mature in their faith.

Dear Jesus, I want to be more like You. Help me to humbly learn from others who want to be like You too. It's in Your name I ask it. Amen.

MILA

A Wonderful Whale

2009

magine taking part in a free-diving competition, hoping to be hired for your dream job. You plunge into a tank containing twenty feet of cold Arctic water. Suddenly, your legs cramp. You can't move them. You panic. As you sink to the bottom of the tank, you choke and gasp from the frigid cold. As this is a free-diving contest, you have no breathing equipment. Scared and frantic, you feel certain you are going to die.

That's what happened to twenty-six-year-old Yang Yun when applying for a job as a whale trainer at the Polar Land theme park in Harbin, China. But Mila, a white beluga whale, came to her rescue! Mila, who lived in the tank with another beluga, seemed to sense Yang Yun's distress. Clamping her jaws gently around the young woman's leg, Mila shoved her to the surface. Belugas feed only on tiny fish and squid, so their teeth are small—Mila's bite didn't hurt the paralyzed woman, who survived the frightening incident without injury.

Spectators who witnessed the incredible rescue credit Mila with saving Yang Yun's life. For her swift, livesaving actions, Mila received a Shining World Hero Award and $500 to purchase her favorite treats. Belugas are social, intelligent creatures known for their playful nature. They also have friendly faces that always appear to be smiling, so Mila looked quite pleased in the publicity photos taken during the award ceremony.

SOMETHING TO THINK ABOUT

Have you ever come to someone's rescue like Mila did? Maybe you helped an anxious friend study for an important test. Perhaps you gave a comforting hug to someone who was crying or held the hand of a small child while helping her to cross the street. If so, that's wonderful! Keep it up! The Bible encourages us to "not become weary in doing good" (Galatians 6:9).

Dear heavenly Father, You are the ultimate Rescuer. You sent Jesus to save us from our sins. You know our every struggle. Thank You for always looking out for us. In Jesus's name, amen.

PATRON

Hero of Ukraine

2022

When Mykhailo Iliev purchased Patron as a pet for his son, the man had no idea that one day the plucky little Jack Russell terrier would capture the heart of the Ukrainian people, becoming a symbol of patriotism and the beloved mascot of the country's State Emergency Service.

Patron (whose name means "ammo" in the Ukrainian language) had been trained to sniff out gunpowder. Now his powerful snout is being used to detect land mines and other undetonated explosive devices brought into Ukraine by Russian soldiers when they invaded in 2022. Wearing a pint-sized protective vest similar to those worn by human members of the team, Patron locates deadly weapons for the bomb squad to defuse. Trained to detect the smell of gunpowder, Patron sniffs and sniffs. He gives a signal when he has located a deadly mine or missile. That's when Iliev and the other men take over. The work is important but tiring too. After successfully locating more than 200 devices, Patron was presented with a medal by Ukraine's President Volodymyr Zelenskyy during a special ceremony. Patron barked and wagged his tail enthusiastically. He seemed to appreciate all the attention. Later, Patron fell asleep during a press conference.

The plucky pup also does charity work, visiting children in schools and hospitals, helping to educate youngsters about weapons. President Zelenskyy said, "Due to the Russian invaders, this is now one of the most urgent tasks—to teach children to recognize and avoid explosive devices."

The frisky, cheese-loving terrier appears regularly on various Ukrainian social media sites. He even has more than 400,000 followers on his Instagram page!

SOMETHING TO THINK ABOUT

Patron was meant to be a house pet. Instead, he is doing important work in Ukraine—work that is tough and tiring.

Some small task God is calling you to do today may lead to something bigger and more important in the future. "Whatever you do, work at it with all your heart, as working for the Lord" (Colossians 3:23).

Heavenly Father, thank You for watching over me from sunrise to sunset and all through the night. Surround me with Your love and peace so that I might bravely follow the path You have planned for me. In Jesus's name, amen.

PELORUS JACK

Guardian Dolphin

1888

Dolphins are friendly, curious, and smart. Really smart. Pelorus Jack was one of the most amazing. He achieved a legendary reputation during his lifetime. Jack appeared one day to guide a steamship through the perilous waters of the French Pass in Pelorus Sound—a dangerous six-mile stretch between New Zealand's two main islands. The pass was known for its treacherous currents, sharp rocks, and shipwrecks. Sailors held their breath as they carefully navigated these perilous waters. But with Jack—a fourteen-foot guardian to lead the way—ships made it safely through. Jack guided ships for twenty-four years. Some estimate that his timely escort may have prevented the deaths of hundreds or perhaps even thousands of people. Others say the dolphin was simply being playful, that he enjoyed riding the high bow waves in front of a speeding ship. He liked to rub against the steel plates of steamships too.

Word quickly spread about the helpful dolphin. Celebrities like Mark Twain and Rudyard Kipling journeyed to New Zealand just to see him. When Jack bounded joyfully through the waves toward a ship, those onboard shouted, "Here comes Pelorus Jack!" Squeaking loudly and waving a fin, Jack would catch the attention of the crew before leading the ship through the treacherous pass to safer waters. Delighted passengers leaned over the ship's railing to watch the dolphin dart and leap through the waves.

Then in 1904, a drunken man aboard the *SS Penguin* tried to shoot the friendly dolphin. Indignant passengers alerted the crew, who restrained and disarmed the shooter. Oddly enough, Pelorus Jack never accompanied the *SS Penguin* again. When the ship sank off the South Wellington Coast in 1909 and all but one passenger drowned, the report of the tragedy reinforced the superstitious rumor that any ship unescorted by Jack would surely sink.

There are several photographs of Jack, who appears to have been a rare albino (white) Risso's dolphin, not common in New Zealand waters. No one knows where he came from. He appeared to be solitary, never swimming with other dolphins. Perhaps he was a lonely orphan. Is that why he sought the company of ships? Or had he witnessed ships sinking and people drowning and wanted to help somehow? No one has been able to explain his unusual behavior. Over the years, as Jack aged, he swam a lot slower and became less energetic. Then one day in 1912, he disappeared, never to be seen again.

SOMETHING TO THINK ABOUT

Over the years, people have honored Pelorus Jack in many ways. Songs and poems have been written about him. A chocolate bar and a ship were named after him. His image serves as the logo for the New Zealand ferry system, and a life-size bronze sculpture of Jack has been erected too.

We have an even more trustworthy guide to lead us safely through life's treacherous passes. Guess who? Jesus, our Lord and Savior!

Thank You, Jesus, for dying on the cross for me. I don't have to worry about sinking in troubled waters. You are our Savior and our trustworthy guide. I believe in You and praise Your name. Amen.

MOLLY

The Magnificent

2005

Molly has a fake leg, just like a storybook pirate! The small gray speckled pony—a cross between an Appaloosa and a Shetland pony—survived the ravages of Hurricane Katrina. Kaye Harris rescued Molly when her owners were forced to abandon their pony in New Orleans to flee the approaching storm. Afterward, Molly was viciously attacked by a pit bull. She suffered injuries to her face, flank, neck, and legs. The dog chewed Molly's right front leg to the bone. Kaye Harris took Molly to a veterinarian. He suggested that euthanizing the pony would be the most humane thing to do. But Kaye insisted that Molly had a strong will to live. So the vet provided Molly with medical care and amputated her injured leg. The determined pony recovered quickly.

When Kaye suggested fitting Molly with a prosthetic (an artificial leg), the vet said the procedure was expensive and difficult and that most animals never adjusted to a fake limb. But Molly wasn't just any ordinary animal. She was sweet natured, intelligent, and spunky. She had an unquenchable spirit. When Molly was finally fitted with a new leg, she coped bravely with the pain and quicky adapted to the prosthetic. Everyone marveled at Molly's courageous spirit.

That's when Kaye had an idea. She began taking Molly to children's hospitals, where the energetic pony serves as a source of inspiration for children with special needs. Her friendly, cheerful manner brings joy to the elderly in nursing homes too. Kaye takes the pony to visit youngsters at cancer camps, where the pony works her "Molly magic" giving hope to others. Although Molly never trained to be a therapy animal, her natural empathy, or ability to share others' feelings, make her an ideal creature for the task.

SOMETHING TO THINK ABOUT

God watches over His animals. Like us, they are His creatures. He helped Molly survive the hurricane, the attack, and the painful surgery. Now this "tough as nails" pony brings hope to others.

The Lord can use you in the same way if you'll let Him. Molly is one of a kind, and so are you.

*Thank You, Lord, for making each of us special
in our own way. In Jesus's name, amen.*

SCARLETT

Fearless Feline Faces the Flames

1996

W hen New York firefighters responded to a call to battle flames at an abandoned garage in Brooklyn, they noticed a stray calico cat rescuing her newborn kittens from the blaze. One at a time the cat darted into the burning building to retrieve a kitten, carry it in her mouth to safety, and then place it gently in a grassy patch nearby. Despite burned paws and ears, the mama kitty continued with her lifesaving mission. Her eyes blistered shut. Her fur became scorched, leaving ugly welts on her bare skin. Since she could no longer see, the cat used her nose to touch each kitten to make sure she'd saved the entire litter. Then she collapsed, unconscious.

Firefighters rushed the feline family to an emergency animal clinic. Scarlett's act of compassion made news around the world. The story of the cat's heroism brought many people to tears. Scores offered the cats a loving home. Karen Wellen was chosen to adopt the mama cat, whom she named Scarlett. Despite her injuries, Scarlett proved to be a happy, loving pet. She liked to play and cuddle. When she passed away in 2008, New Yorkers gave Scarlett a hero's farewell by broadcasting her image on the Jumbotron in Times Square. Scarlett's heroism lives on. The

North Shore Animal League created an award in her honor—the Scarlett Award for Animal Heroism.

SOMETHING TO THINK ABOUT

Despite her pain and injuries, Scarlett lived her life to the fullest. We can be like Scarlett too. Life is a gift from God. We should cherish it. Always remember that God loves you. Take these words into your heart: "'I know the plans I have for you,' declares the LORD, 'plans to prosper you and not to harm you, plans to give you hope and a future'" (Jeremiah 29:11).

Dear heavenly Father, thank You for loving me and planning good things for my life. In Jesus's name, amen.

ABOUT THE AUTHOR

Shirley Raye Redmond is an award-winning writer and newspaper columnist. Her many books include *Courageous and Bold Bible Heroes*, *Brave Heroes and Bold Defenders*, and *Courageous World Changers*, which won a 2021 *Christianity Today* book award. She is also a sought-after workshop speaker and a member of the Society of Children's Book Writers and Illustrators.

DISCOVER SOME OF GOD'S GREATEST HEROES!

You can learn about some incredible men and women who used their God-given gifts and amazing talents to change history. These real-life superheroes risked it all to save others, stand up for what's right, and spread the good news of Jesus around the world.

HEROES AREN'T BORN – THEY ARE MADE

None of these people started out as courageous world changers or bold defenders, but each one chose to follow God wherever He led them. Guess what? God has awesome plans for you too! All you need to do is say yes to Him to begin your life-changing adventure.

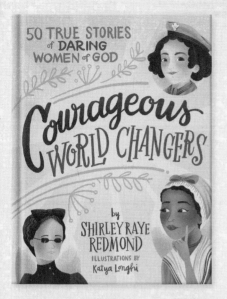
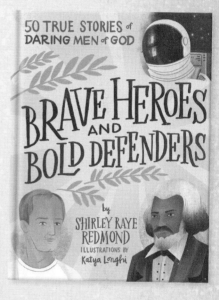
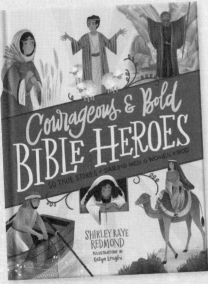